GET THE JOB

You really <u>want</u>

IN A POST-PANDEMIC WORLD

DELLA JUDD

Copyright © 2022 by Della Judd. All rights reserved.

This book or any portion thereof may not be reproduced or used in any manner whatsoever without the express written permission of the publisher except for the use of brief quotations in a book review.

Strenuous attempts have been made to credit all copyrighted materials used in this book. All such materials and trademarks, which are referenced in this book, are the full property of their respective copyright owners. Any omissions will be rectified in future editions.

Cover image by: Raffy Ferras Hoylar, 99Designs
Book design by: SWATT Books Ltd

Printed in the United Kingdom
First Printing, 2022

ISBN: 978-0-904373-21-9 (Paperback)
ISBN: 978-0-904373-22-9 (eBook)

SYNJON Books
Ampthill, Milton Keynes

Praise

'This book would easily be digested by someone who might have been out of the job market for a long time, such as someone whose role has been made redundant.' — **Megan Rowe, Lead People Partner**

'This book is like having a coach in your pocket — on-tap, 24/7, whether you're sitting down and planning your next career move or just want to take stock and reflect. The book contains highly practical actions and activities to support you every step of the way — even once you've started your dream job.' — **Hannah Erskine, Assessment and Development Centre Manager**

'This is an indispensable guide on how to get your dream role. Della takes you through every aspect of work, supporting you to identify what you want and need from your next job and providing you with reassurance and practical exercises to help you secure the move that's right for you. An excellent guide that will help all those looking to change their working lives for the better.' — **Alison McNamara, Chief People Officer**

'This book is a great guide for anyone wishing to achieve the career they strive for. It should be a book you can use over and over. A book you can refer back to. It will help you consider your options, look at yourself and think differently. A must for anyone who has their dream job in mind.' — **Helen Joyce, Recruitment Director**

'Our lives are all very different and take many twists and turns, however how often do you make a genuine investment in yourself? Give yourself the time and space to work through Della's *Get the Job You Really Want in a Post-Pandemic World* and it will provide you with a personal bible for life, both now and for the future. Della's many experiences can provide you with inspiration, guidance and focus to get you to pinpoint what really matters to you and how you can make it happen. I look forward to revisiting this book time and time again.' — **Lindsay O'Kane, Senior Tax Manager**

'Della helped me to work through my work problems and identify what I wanted from my future role. Providing me with helpful tips and examples, I built up the skills and confidence to carry on in my role, whilst focussing on my career search with a better understanding of my ideal job checklist Several months later, I found my new role, and went into my new role with greater confidence.' — **Jack Richards, Recruitment and Resourcing Manager**

'Della helped me to gain clarity to take the next steps in my career journey, which seemed hard at first, but became manageable when I had the right information on my side. I am now in a new role which I would not have applied for without Della's expertise.' — **Project Manager**

'Using Della's exercises was a real turning point for me. I am now happily contracting doing a role I enjoy that offers me a great challenge, and even better is double the money I was on. I am no longer in a role that drains me, working for managers that made me feel worthless.' — **Recruitment Manager**

Other comments:

'The difference in my health is amazing — I would probably have had a breakdown if I had to carry on in that role.'

'The ideal job planner was crucial and made me focus my energy on what I like, not what I tolerate.'

'Interview prep section was brilliant as it enabled me to sell myself but also to interview the company itself to see if it was what I wanted. I was able to secure three roles thinking like this which increased my confidence hugely and also made me realise what I was actually good at.'

'The exercises made me think about the job search differently because it made me question my approach when looking for my ideal job, how I approached my search. They showed me not to settle for a lesser role than I was striving for.'

'This approach 100% helped me get my new role. I was extremely low when I started, and I could not see what future I wanted. It changed my way of thinking, my approach, and the way I conducted myself at interview — head held high and confident.'

'I can't thank Della enough for how she changed my thinking, helped me move on and get rid of the history I was feeling and also for bringing my spark back to life when I thought I was rubbish and low. Thank you so much for everything you did.'

'My confidence and self-belief is a lot stronger since following the exercises.'

Contents

Acknowledgements	7
Foreword	9
Prologue	11
Chapter 1 – My story	13
Chapter 2 – Introduction	15
Chapter 3 – Why are you here?	27
Chapter 4 – Who are you?	59
Chapter 5 – Digging deeper	75
Chapter 6 – Designing your dream job – what do you want?	91
Chapter 7 – What am I good at?	119
Chapter 8 – Creating your ideal job checklist	147
Chapter 9 – Telling others	157
Chapter 10 – Letting go of the past	167
Chapter 11 – Planning your search	177
Chapter 12 – Making the application	189
Chapter 13 – Feeling confident – before, during and after	203
Chapter 14 – Getting the role / Interviews	223
Chapter 15 – Accepting the offers (or not)	243
Chapter 16 – Congratulations	253
Chapter 17 – More case studies	267
About the author	271
Bonus chapters and free stuff!	273

DELLA JUDD

Acknowledgements

IT'S BEEN A great journey writing my first business book and there are plenty of people to thank along the way.

Sarah Hamilton-Gill — for telling me to just get on with it
Karen Williams, the Book Mentor — for her mentoring support and deadlines
Charlie Neary — for the push to get people to see the book
Sam Pearce from SWATT books — for making the book look amazing
Louise Lubke Cuss — for her editorial support

My early readers: Megan Rowe, Lindsay O'Kane, Karen Kipling, Hannah Erskine, Anna Skelton, Issy Harvey, Alison McNamara, Helen Joyce

My family for their comments, insights, and support: Neal Judd, Louie Judd and Daniel Judd

All the people I have ever worked with, and all my coaching clients from whom I have got so much inspiration

Thank you for buying the book. By buying the book you are already supporting another jobseeker in need. Through my crowdfunding project a Buy One, Donate One scheme was created where over 50 books were donated to Key Business Skills Ltd, a charity based in Milton Keynes and Northampton. For every 10 books purchased another book will be donated to the scheme.

Foreword

I WISH I had this book years ago when I was made redundant following my maternity leave after the birth of my daughter. I'd spent years building my career, managing teams, and investing all my time and headspace in my job. It was all I knew. Then suddenly becoming a parent and losing my job was a huge shock. I knew I wanted to work but my head was swimming with confusion and questions. Did I even want to go back to the career I'd had? Was that who I was now? I knew I wanted to work, but I also wanted to be there for my family. I wanted both, a career and a family, but the workplace didn't feel set up for people like me.

Fast forward 10 years and here we are now. As the Founder of Flexible Working People, I have built a community of over 40k people who want to find a better way and find work that works for them.

I met the author of this book, Della Judd, through the community, and through our shared passion for flexible working and supporting people to navigate the world of work and find and get jobs they love. Through her work as a coach Della helps people to find out what it is that drives them, how to find a job that's right for them and how to match their passions to their job role, improving their lives and ultimately making them happier.

One of the most frequently discussed topics in the Flexible Working People community is from people who need support through job change. People who feel lost and confused, who have fallen out of love with their career, who are looking for a way back into the workplace after a career break or who simply want to find that elusive work-life balance.

The pandemic has had a seismic impact on the workplace and on people's attitudes and needs relating to their work. For many it has been the catalyst for change with people questioning what they really want from their career and what's important to them. No longer are people accepting the status quo

— the 9-5, the office being the only place that you can work. And companies are re-writing the rule books with the birth of hybrid working and increase in flexible and remote work.

In this book Della uses her coaching system and techniques to ask people to think about what they really want, to dig a bit deeper into their passions and their whys and how to confidently present themselves to get the job they really want. And that's the key... It's not just about deciding what you want to do but also how you are going to be successful in securing a job that you love. Della takes you on a step-by-step journey from working out what it is that you want to do (or not do!), that plays to your passions, strengths and skills, as well as how are you going to translate that into securing a job that's going to make you happy. With practical advice, guidance and exercises this book is like having a coach by your side.

As we emerge out of one of the most overwhelming and life changing periods in our lifetime, this book offers the help and support that is so needed if you are navigating your way from confusion to happiness at work.

Katy Fridman — Founder, Flexible Working People

Prologue

THE PANDEMIC HIT us all for six when it landed in 2020. By March, most of the world was in a lockdown situation. At first there was shock, panic (panic buying of many toilet rolls), worry and fear. Then, slowly, as we started to get used to this enforced period of staying at home without a commute, of spending more time with our families, of focussing on the things that really mattered, we started to question what had gone before.

Why were we living in this rat race of commuting, of racing out of the door to pick up our kids, of presentism, trying to prove that by being in the office for longer hours we were somehow achieving more? Why were we spending more time with our colleagues than with our families? Why not get a dog and get outside for our daily exercise? Why not take up that hobby with the two hours that would normally be spent on the packed 18.03 out of Euston? Why not indeed?

And then when the 'return to office' plans started to emerge different businesses had different approaches. Some said, 'Work where you like — we trust you', some said, 'We'd like you back in the office because we can see the benefits of collaboration, but you can choose what works', and others said, 'We want you back in, we want to see you, we want you back in on these days, no matter what'.

And suddenly there was a realisation that perhaps we didn't all want to work how our organisations were telling us to work. Perhaps we didn't want to go back. Perhaps we wanted to go forward with some new way.

Certainly, the reflection time that the last two years have provided has given many of us space to think, time to breathe. Time to wake up and smell the coffee. Time to focus on what we really want in life and from work.

We have seen how a hybrid, more flexible approach to work can be. We've seen it, we've lived it and many of us have liked it. Whatever your reason for looking for a job you really want, there are choices out there. There are more choices than before — as businesses start to rework their recruitment strategies, look at their benefits packages and focus on culture as a major driver for retention.

The post-pandemic world is going to look very, very different. How will your world look?

Chapter 1
My story

'**IT MIGHT BE** meningitis,' said the manager of my son's nursery.

At that moment my heart stopped, and everything changed.

They said that the tell-tale spots were not disappearing when they did the glass test. I asked them to call my husband and get my son to A and E for assessment. I grabbed my bag and ran.

I was about to embark on one of the longest drives of my life. The drive seemed longer, the traffic seemed busier, the route seemed endless.

When I arrived at the hospital, they were doing all manner of tests and it turned out to be an allergic reaction. I felt sick all the way there, and guilt-ridden that I wasn't there for him.

A few weeks later I was offered a promotion to senior manager and a significant pay rise. All I could think about was my family, and I knew that I couldn't be that far away, no matter how much money was at stake.

At the time I was working for a large publishing organisation, on good money and with the promotion on offer. I was thriving and doing really well. I'd made a big impact. Teams were productive, morale was improving, I was getting plaudits from my boss.

The only trouble was the 90-minute drive to the office on a daily basis. Every day I left before the kids got up and arrived home just in time for bedtime. I put a teabag in a cup for my husband to show that

I'd thought of him before I left. I worked hard in the evening doing bottles, laundry and prep to show that I was contributing as a mother.

After this scare I started to think about what was really important in life. What did I really want? I knew that at that moment in time, I needed to put my family first. Careers can go down as well as up.

I remember talking about getting a job more locally and sacrificing salary over closeness. To me the extra salary and promotion wasn't worth it. That moment was the catalyst for me. I turned down the promotion and looked at what I really wanted instead. I started to explore local opportunities. I went back to basics and looked at the type of job I wanted and where it needed to be.

My first **'ideal job checklist'** was being created. I wanted to be nearer home. I wanted to see my kids in the morning and do the school and nursery run. I wanted to be available for teatime and story time and cuddles. I realised that the long commute was making me miss out on so much. The salary, the status, the opportunity just wasn't worth it.

Talking to my husband about it was hard. He's an accountant, driven by success, but also my real cheerleader who has always made sure that I know my own worth. He was certain that I could operate at the more senior level — I'd done it before. I was able and I was being fast tracked. Why didn't I want it? I had to explain how I felt and how what I really wanted at this moment in time was my family. And it made me realise the importance of bringing other people along on the journey with you. After all it wasn't just about me.

After a few weeks I found a job which was less than 10 minutes' drive from my house. It meant a grade drop and a salary drop. I gained 10 hours a week to be with my family.

Once I made the change, my life changed significantly. I was able to do the school run, the nursery run, see my children. I could eat breakfast with them, read them stories and be a much more present part of their life. Eventually I was able to work my way back up to director level as the children got older. Careers can bounce back.

I had a choice to make: take the bigger salary and the bigger job or come home and be near my family. It is a decision I have never regretted.

I am now an ICF accredited coach, having taken my diploma after my role was made redundant in 2018. I was offered a move to a global role, one that would require me to live out of a suitcase for two weeks out of four. Despite my children getting older, I realised that as teenagers they had just as many requirements as when they were toddlers, and I wanted to be around for those moments. They still wanted my presence and my support. And I wanted to be there.

Chapter 2

Introduction

WELCOME! YOU ARE about to start the process of exploring how to get the job you REALLY want. This book follows the coaching model that I use with my high-end executive clients, and it goes deeper than just writing your CV and getting you any old job.

This process digs deep. You explore what you really want. And I mean REALLY! You might never have told anyone else what you REALLY want before.

Maybe you've had ideas of what you'd like to do for years and have suppressed them. 'Society says I should do this.' 'Family says I should do that.' Peer pressure. Money worries. Obligation. There are many reasons why we take jobs we don't really want, and then we wake up one day and realise we feel stuck, bored, unwell or unhappy. Or maybe all of those!

But you know you are not satisfied. You know there is more, that you want more. You want a job that is actually enjoyable. Purposeful. Fun. You want to work with great people. People that get you. A boss that values you. A boss that says thank you and challenges you.

Maybe you want to be able to learn and develop your skills? Perhaps you want to turn up and add more value than you do right now? You certainly want to feel that you have done a fabulous job.

You might have years of experience which you want to use without apologising.

You'd prefer to turn up, be yourself, deliver great results, live your purpose, achieve things, get a buzz, and go home happy, rather than putting on a brave new face every time you log on or go to work, which leaves you exhausted, stressed, and burnt out.

Maybe you feel that your face doesn't fit, or you don't feel comfortable where you are at?

Maybe you don't like the direction of travel that the organisation is taking. You might be feeling pressure because of restructures, reorganisations, or new management.

You know you want to move on, but perhaps you're paralysed with fear about getting the next job move wrong. You don't want a frying pan into fire situation! Maybe you feel stuck, and you are struggling to get motivated to move on to better things.

Maybe you have realised that life is too short, and you want to spend time with your family. You know you are giving more energy to work you dislike than to your family. But it's the only thing you can do to get by at the moment.

Maybe you want to be able to leave the job behind at the end of the day, knowing that no-one is expecting you to check your emails every five minutes, where you can create a more balanced life, where you feel energised, not exhausted. Not stressed with the clash of your life and the work you do. Hell, you want time for A life. Some hobbies might be nice. Some time to chill in the evening.

You want to get to Friday and have some energy to go out and have fun, not collapse with exhaustion, drink too much and numb yourself with TV until Sunday.

You want a Sunday where you can truly switch off and not be second-guessing your Monday. Where you are not trying to get ahead or trying to rev yourself up for the week ahead. Where you don't have to brace yourself and paint your face on to be a person you're not for the next five days.

You want something different. You want to find an organisation that is a great fit.

Currently you don't feel like that.

There is another way. You can take some time to reflect and get the job you REALLY want. There will be a job, an organisation, a leader, that gets you. That wants you for YOU. That needs your unique set of skills and style, ethos, and personality.

You need to know what you want, what those skills are and what your ethos is. Then you can go and find it.

Ready? Let's start.

Take some time to write down everything that is going on for you right now. What challenges are you experiencing, and what reasons are you looking for a new role?

Input destination

If you were planning a long train trip you wouldn't just turn up to the station and jump on the first train that pulled in, yet that is exactly what many of us do with a job search. Type in our job title, see a role and apply for it. And then wonder why we are in the wrong place, with the wrong people at the wrong time.

To get the destination we really want we need to make a plan.

Think like a trip:

Why are you going? To relax, to explore?

Where do you want to go? Somewhere warm? Somewhere familiar? Good food? Is it remote or bustling?

How do we want to travel? What type of service? Backpacking or first class?

What is our budget? What can we afford to spend (or earn)?

What sort of people do we want to be around? Club 18–30 party vibe or sophisticated adult-only luxury?

Job searching is hard work! It takes a huge amount of effort and time. Emotionally as well as physically. So doing the groundwork now will help you to establish your ultimate destination and will save time, effort, and energy.

I believe that by doing up-front thinking and planning, you can ensure that you are only applying for jobs that you really want. Only looking at jobs that are relevant, only attending interviews with companies that you know you would love to get an offer from. If you are looking for an internal move, planning your next steps and approach can be just as valuable as if you are looking to go to somewhere new. Checking that your existing organisation is the BEST match for you right now is a worthwhile exercise and can ensure that your internal move is just as successful as moving to a new organisation.

This book will help you to create your **ideal job checklist** before you start your search.

You'll explore the work you want from lots of different angles — including what your values are, what your dream job might look like, and what sort of family balance you want. By the time you start your search you'll know exactly what you are looking for so your search can be tailored and specific.

Once you start applying, you'll know exactly what to be putting in your CV to make it stand out. During interviews, you'll know exactly what stories and case studies to focus on to show how you are the right fit for the organisation.

What you will get from this book

You've bought the book, now what?

Whilst I can't promise that you will get a 100% match with every single aspect of a job you want, I will take you on a step-by-step process to getting a much better match than you have right now.

You will learn about yourself. You will be asking yourself (and answering) some questions that maybe you have simply never asked yourself before. Maybe you have a deep-down desire to do something different in work but have never actually given yourself the time to explore that vision.

What could a dream job look like?

What could your life look like if you were doing something you loved (or at least really liked) every day?

I believe that too many of us are in jobs we dislike. 60% of people leave a job because of a bad boss and 41% of people are looking to change jobs, according to a global Microsoft survey.[1] It means that many of us are looking for things to change and are maybe just in work because 'we have to pay the bills' or 'because we just fell into it'.

> *I didn't expect to be an electricity industry expert by the time I was 27 but I had become one, simply because of the first job I took after university. Was it what I really wanted? No — not at that stage. I had to take time later on to think about my ideal job, my values, the work-life balance I wanted to achieve. I had to get to a breaking point before I took the time to reflect and make the change.*

I believe that if you get a job that better matches your values, your skills, your passions then you become happier, less stressed, and healthier. You will be better at that job, because you are so aligned to it, attuned to the purpose. You'll be using your natural talents and your existing skills and personality, so you will excel, your confidence will grow, and you will achieve better results.

---

[1] The Great Resignation: How employers drove workers to quit, BBC Worklife, 1 July 2021, https://www.bbc.com/worklife/article/20210629-the-great-resignation-how-employers-drove-workers-to-quit

You'll have the balance in your life that you are dreaming of; you'll be spending time where you want to be spending it: with your kids, with your pets, with your family, playing sport, doing hobbies, travelling. Whatever it is you are wishing you had more of, you can create a plan right now to get it.

Along the way you'll also learn more about what makes you tick. You will understand your values, your purpose in life and work. You'll understand what part work plays in your life right now and what is important to you.

You'll get a view about your own work style, and if you're a leader, your ethos and management style. You'll be able to say, *'This is me, I lead like this, I work like this, I want to be doing this, I love this, I am passionate about this'*.

Importantly, you will also explore what you don't like!

Sometimes reflecting on what aspects of work you *don't* like can be as enlightening as exploring what you *do* want.

In fact, many of you won't know yet what you want. And that is perfectly normal!

But you do know that you are not happy with where you are right now, you know the sort of boss you don't want, the sort of co-workers you don't want to work with. This is good information, and you'll start to explore those aspects to build a bigger picture of what you like and don't like, then you can get focussed on getting the job you really want. You might be in an organisation that feels right, but you are looking for something else in a role. You might choose to use this guide to work out what you want to apply for internally which would be a more suitable alternative.

Throughout the book there will be exercises for you to complete. There will also be case studies dotted throughout. I'll also be sharing my own stories *(in italics)* and some of the key turning points that I made during my career.

You will be creating your **ideal job checklist** — a checklist for the job that matches the vision you want. You'll also know what your non-negotiables are — what aspects of any offer you will be more flexible with and what the absolute 'no ways' are!

This is a workbook-style guide and I'd recommend that you make notes as you go whether in the book itself or in your own journal if you like more freedom to scrawl and doodle!

Thinking is good, but we will cover a lot — so make notes of any thoughts or epiphanies that come up! During the book I'll encourage you to go back and review some of the reflections as you build your ultimate **ideal job checklist**.

Take your time.

This is a book I would encourage you not to rush through and finish in one sitting. It will take some time, and you might find that you only have enough energy or brain space to do one exercise at a time. This is fine! In fact, sometimes the reflections we make and the thoughts that come up after an exercise can be really valuable, and these thoughts sometimes take a bit of time to surface.

You might see this logo pop up at various points — this is where I would encourage a 'PAUSE POINT', time for a cuppa and reflection time. At the end of each chapter there is a summary of everything we have covered, and I'd encourage you to check you've not missed anything, have a break and let yourself have some thinking time.

There are a LOT of exercises and a LOT of questions. Don't feel like you have to answer them all. Don't feel like there is an answer for everything; some questions will be more relevant to you than others. If you feel like 'this doesn't apply to me', then simply skip it and move on. If you don't have the time or capacity to give a section proper thought right now, then mark it and return to it when you do have time.

Some sections you might want to go back over to see what you came up with, and as you build your **ideal job checklist** and start to reach conclusions about your search, I'll be asking you to revisit the answers you gave to various sections so you can gather all of the knowledge together.

I'd recommend you use the sections within the book to write things down as you go along. You'll want to look back at the notes you make as it starts to shape the thinking later on.

Here's what we will do. There are some key sections to the book.

The first section is about WHY you are here, WHY now? We'll explore a variety of potential reasons why you are looking to change now. Knowing WHY can help you focus.

Next is all about exploring WHO you are; what experiences make up the unique individual that makes you, YOU? We'll explore your values, your experience of culture and work purpose.

Then, we'll start to get creative. You're going to be thinking about the job you really want, the hours you want to work, the location you want to be in. You're going to be writing down the sorts of organisation you want to work for, the type of culture it has and the people you want to work with. You'll think about what you don't want too!

We'll explore WHAT skills you have, WHAT you are naturally talented at. We'll be working out what things about work you find easy, what you are passionate about and what tasks and elements you'd rather avoid.

Once you've done your big thinking you will then start to build your **ideal job checklist** and start to hone your search. This is where you can start to be really focussed about your applications and the companies you'd like to work for. This step is crucial as you'll start to make decisions about what to apply for and what not to apply for. Here you will get laser focussed.

You'll need to sell yourself to the best advantage once you've identified your dream job — so the next section is all about creating your CV, showing off your skills and presenting what it is about YOU that makes you different from everyone else.

Once you start applying, then the final section is all about presenting your best self, being confident and showing your passions. This is THE job you really want — so you want to make sure you're passionate about it and selling yourself to the best of your ability.

Take time to work through each section — get your checklist ready and then have it with you as you review job descriptions, make applications, and review your offers.

Remember, this is a detailed, in-depth assessment of all aspects of your work, skills and life. It will take some time and require some deep thinking. Take regular breaks and reflect on the exercises as they come up.

 **Exercise**

Key Date Planner

Now you know what we will cover, it could be helpful to start to plan. Note down any key drivers and dates that initially come to mind about your job search.

_____

_____

_____

_____

Things to consider:

- When do you want a new job by — realistically?
- If your role is being made redundant, what dates are you working to?
- If you are returning to work (perhaps after a break or maternity leave), what are the key dates?
- Note down any key dates that you are already aware of.

_____

_____

_____

_____

Ideal new start date: _____

What your notice period is (if any): _____

Planning ahead

Any up-front work you do now will save you hours of wasted applications or interviews later. It often feels easy to start our search by logging onto a job site and seeing what is there. Before we know it we have clicked on three jobs and applied with the 'easy apply' button without considering the organisation, the culture or whether it would actually work for us.

To get the best use from this workbook, I'd encourage you to take a little bit of time to plan how you might use it and when you can do the exercises.

Think about how much time you can spend on this each day / week. Make a note in your calendar to take time out to do this preparation stage. After all, this is about getting the job you really want, not just getting any old job.

Use the space below to make a note of anything that you need to do to prepare your time and space so you can dedicate the time you need to this process. Note down what time you can spend, when you can commit to specific times using the workbook and doing your search.

_____

_____

_____

Note down what needs to happen to allow that to take place consistently. What help might you need?

_____

_____

_____

Finally, make a commitment to yourself that you will do the work. Don't feel tempted to skip through the chapters and read it in one sitting. Do the exercises; absorb the information that comes up from your thinking. Make notes so you remember what you take away from each exercise. Then move on to the next exercise, the next chapter.

Try to avoid doing the job search at the same time. Chances are you will spend wasted time on a search that isn't targeted. Give yourself a week or two, stop the searches, stop applying for new roles and really focus on this project. Then at the other end, you will know what you really want to apply for and can go for it with energy and enthusiasm.

It's time to take stock. It's time to work for an organisation that makes you feel good.

How will it feel when you get a job you are right for?

How do you feel now?

On a scale of 1 to 10, score how you feel right now about the job you have.

1	2	3	4	5	6	7	8	9	10
It's as bad as it can be				OK					Can't be better

Make a note along the line. We'll review the score later when you start applying for other roles, and when you get a new one.

 **Summary**

Get prepared to make sure you get the most out of this book.

1. Make sure you have a notebook if you don't want to write in this book!

2. Think about your destination — where do you want to be heading?

3. Make a plan so you know what time you have.

4. Commit some time to this process; you'll save time and energy in the weeks ahead!

5. Score how you currently feel about your present (or last) role.

Chapter 3

Why are you here?

WHY ARE YOU looking for a new opportunity?

You are not alone. According to a survey carried out by Randstad UK at the end of 2021, 69% of people were reported to be 'ready' to change role and 25% said they were looking to change within three to six months; this is compared to normal levels of 11%.

> 'Almost a quarter of workers are actively planning to change employers in the next few months, a report has claimed, as part of a "great resignation" prompted by a high number of vacancies and burnout caused by the pandemic.'[2]

There might be a whole host of reasons why you are looking for a new opportunity and we'll explore some of them here. It's important to know why you are looking for something different, so that you don't just jump into another opportunity that looks sexy and exciting but essentially is just the same or causing similar problems as before.

As you read the following sections, put a big tick in the tick box at the end of each section for any of the reasons that resonate with you. It will help you to see what your driver(s) is/are for moving on. If

---

[2] The Great Resignation, Randstad UK, https://www.randstad.co.uk/about-us/industry-insight/great-resignation/ quoted in The Guardian, 1 November 2021, www.theguardian.com/money/2021/nov/01/the-great-resignation-almost-one-in-four-workers-planning-job-change

you know why you are keen to explore new opportunities or work for a different type of organisation, it can help you to make sure you don't pick the same role or type of organisation again.

There are also questions for you to ponder as you work through each section. If you've ticked one particular area, make sure that you think about the questions or do the exercise with it. Use the space provided to jot down any thoughts that come up or write in your notebook. You'll come back to these later as you create your **ideal job checklist**.

Hybrid working, flexibility and balance

A new way of working has emerged. It's called hybrid. It's here to stay and yet it is an unknown entity. Companies and leaders haven't yet decided what it is and what they want it to be.

'A hybrid model of working allows employees to blend working from different locations such as home, office or normal place of work.'[3]

Employers are responding to the changes in rules and opening up their offices and businesses once more, but the variety of approaches is vast. There is no one-size-fits-all in this new world. Businesses will be adapting their strategy (or not), and the organisation that you've been working for might be changing in ways that you don't like.

In an Office of National Statistics survey 81% of employees asked said that they wanted a hybrid solution when the pandemic was over, and 33% would look for new work if they didn't have a choice about where they work.[4]

Perhaps this is you? Perhaps you have successfully worked from home during lockdowns and in the periods following?

You have shown your dedication and your ability to still deliver, meet deadlines and achieve goals. Perhaps you found you were even more productive without constant interruptions, time spent hanging

---

[3] Definition from the Office of National Statistics, https://www.ons.gov.uk/employmentandlabourmarket/peopleinwork/employmentandemployeetypes/articles/businessandindividualattitudestowardsthefutureofhomeworkinguk/apriltomay2021

[4] Business and individual attitudes towards the future of homeworking, UK: April to May 2021, Office of National Statistics, https://www.ons.gov.uk/employmentandlabourmarket/peopleinwork/employmentandemployeetypes/articles/businessandindividualattitudestowardsthefutureofhomeworkinguk/apriltomay2021

around the coffee machine and wasted time chatting after meetings? Or perhaps you miss those 'corridor catch-ups', where you found out in a more informal way what was going on in the office?

Things to consider:

Are you happy with the arrangements your employer is making?

Have they said you can work how you really want to?

Are you having to make compromises?

What did the pandemic show you about the culture of your workplace; were they supportive and helpful, concerned about your health and welfare? Or did they think you were 'shirking at home' and just needed to 'work a bit harder'?

Do you still want to work the way they want you to work?

Can you return to work in a way that works for you?

Perhaps you were enjoying the fact that you could save thousands of pounds on your commute and coffee habit. Or maybe you've gained an hour in bed or at the gym? Perhaps you can save money on childcare support because you can now do the school run and spend more time with the children.

Hybrid working is about the blend of locations but maybe you need flexibility too. Flexibility to start a little later, finish a little earlier. Go to the gym some mornings and have time to shower before turning your laptop on. Maybe you want an organisation that is not tied to the clock-watching culture. One that is flexible when kids or parents are unwell. One that goes with the flow when teenagers need picking up during study leave.

Just as a one-size-fits-all *'work in the office'* policy didn't work for everyone, so a permanent *'work from home'* policy won't work for everyone either.

Many people have been left feeling isolated, and just as many people want to return to the office as those who want to stay at home. If your organisation has declared that they are going to be permanently home working, then that might not be right for you.

Things to consider:

Are you thinking there has to be more to life? Do you want a more balanced life where life comes first — not work?

Are you wanting more time in the office?

Are your boundaries better in the office?

When you go into the office, what do you want to go in for?

Are you able to choose the type of work you do and where you do it?

Where are you the most productive?

What do you like about being in the office?

What do you like about being at home?

Would you like to collaborate more if the environment was suitable?

> 'Given the choice, more than half of employee respondents (54%) would choose flexibility in when they work. By comparison, 40% want flexibility in where they work.'[5]

Work-life balance is something that is talked about but is very hard to achieve. Especially nowadays when technology means that the office is always in our pocket, no matter where we are. Boundaries have become blurred, and many people are striving to get a 'balance' between work, family, and general life. If this is you, then you need to know what BALANCE looks like for you. We will explore that as we go forward. Tick below any of the boxes that apply to you.

BALANCE ☐

FLEXIBLE ☐

HYBRID ☐

OFFICE ☐

---

[5] More than half of employees globally would quit their jobs if not provided post-pandemic flexibility, EY survey finds, EY Global, https://www.ey.com/en_gl/news/2021/05/more-than-half-of-employees-globally-would-quit-their-jobs-if-not-provided-post-pandemic-flexibility-ey-survey-finds

 **Exercise**

Hybrid Working, Flexibility and Balance

Consider these questions and make any notes.

Why do you want to move?

_____

_____

_____

What is it about the current role / previous role regarding working hours / location that makes you want to move on?

_____

_____

_____

What blend do you want? Two days at home, or all at home? Part time?

_____

_____

Why do you want that? Is it to spend more time with the family? Health? Less stress?

_____

_____

_____

What would you want from a new organisation?

_____

_____

_____

_____

Money / Promotion / Dead man's shoes

You might be looking to move on to get further up the ladder. You want to get different experience. Maybe you want to move to a bigger organisation for greater opportunities, or maybe a smaller one where you can be a bigger fish in a smaller pond. Maybe you know that the role you want at your current organisation isn't going to be available — because the person in it currently isn't going anywhere.

Knowing this can be really helpful because you know that ambition lies at the heart of your search. Ambition to earn more, take on more responsibility, learn new tasks. It's worth taking note of so that your new search identifies exactly the criteria you are looking for in an organisation and a role. There's no point moving to another similar size set-up where the same problem will present itself in two years' time. If this applies to you then tick the box below.

PROMOTION ☐

 **Exercise**

Promotion

Where do you want to be in 3 or 5 years' time?

What is the ultimate goal?

What would that role look like?

What skills do you need to gather up along the way?

Where might be a good place to start?

_____

_____

_____

_____

I'm not where I SHOULD be

Sometimes we have family pressures and expectations which can lie heavy on us. Even from childhood, our parents can expect us to achieve certain things and have a particular career. It can leave us feeling that we should be somewhere different, even when we might be happy where we are right now. Perhaps you have taken a career path because of family pressure and are finding that you are in a place which doesn't suit you, which is causing you stress, and you'd really rather be somewhere else.

Things to consider:

What expectations have you had to live with?

_____

_____

_____

What choices have you made that are from a cultural or family perspective?

_____

_____

_____

What stories have you heard about where you SHOULD be in your life?

_____
_____
_____

Are you feeling like you should be doing something else?

_____
_____
_____
_____

Is that a driver for you to move in a new direction now?

_____
_____

If these reasons resonate with you, then tick below:

SHOULD BE SOMEWHERE ELSE ☐

Stress – it's becoming too much

Are you feeling stressed, worn out, overwhelmed by everything that has been thrown at you? Have you had a proper break recently? Are you able to get away and log off and switch off? Do you want more time to yourself?

Stress can be a good thing; in fact, we need a little stress to get us out of bed in the morning. However, when stress levels become pervasive, when they affect your health or other parts of your life, then it can be time to act. If stress is a key concern for you, then tick the box below.

STRESS ☐

I realised that stress was a reason for me wanting to change role when I stopped sleeping through the night. I kept waking at 3 or 4 every morning. The to-do list was running through my head. I would play out every conversation I had yesterday and would play out everything that I thought was going to happen today or tomorrow. I was on high alert, and it affected my whole life. My migraines became chronic, a daily occurrence that left me groggy, tired, and unable to enjoy life.

Exercise

Stress

What symptoms of stress are you showing?

___

___

___

___

What is it, specifically, that is causing you stress?

___

___

___

___

___

Things to consider:

Take some time to assess all aspects of your role and work out in detail what it is that is causing you stress.

Some prompts to help you think:

- Timekeeping — e.g. clock watching
- Deadlines — real or imagined
- Targets — realistic or not
- Reporting — deadlines / creating / writing
- Data / Stats
- Budgets / finance
- People — peers / team members / leader
- Clients — winning them / serving them / complaints
- Physical environment / office space / air con / people you work next to
- Bullying / Harassment / Discrimination
- Travel to and from the office
- Location
- Workload
- Time management — overload / lack of respect for your time / meeting clashes
- Something else?

Is everything work related or are there some aspects of home life that are adding to the stress?

_____

_____

Make a note of everything that comes up.

_____

_____

_____

_____

Health / Burnout

Without our health we don't have anything. I think that the pandemic has shown us that more than anything else. It has, for many, brought into sharp focus the adage that *'Life is too short'* and that *'We only get one life'*.

The mental health charity, MIND, reported that nearly 65% of people felt that their mental health had suffered during the initial stages of lockdown.[6] That's on top of the pre-pandemic stats that estimate that 1 in 4 of us will experience a mental health issue in our lifetime.[7] According to the Mental Health Foundation, 13% of all sick days are attributable to mental health.[8]

Is health one of the reasons you are looking for a change?

Perhaps you are feeling low, unfit, or unhealthy. Perhaps you are perfectly well but have seen others around you fall ill and even lose their lives prematurely? What symptoms are you experiencing that you are ignoring?

Do you have a diagnosed condition or disability? Do you want to work for an organisation that is more inclusive and supportive?

If your health is a concern, you are suffering from or think you might be heading towards burnout, then tick the box.

HEALTH ☐

---

[6] Coronavirus: the consequences for mental health, MIND, July 2021, https://www.mind.org.uk/media/8962/the-consequences-of-coronavirus-for-mental-health-final-report.pdf

[7] How common are mental health problems?, MIND, https://www.mind.org.uk/information-support/types-of-mental-health-problems/statistics-and-facts-about-mental-health/how-common-are-mental-health-problems/

[8] Mental health statistics: mental health at work, Mental Health Foundation, https://www.mentalhealth.org.uk/statistics/mental-health-statistics-mental-health-work

Exercise

Health

Why is health important to you — what does good health mean to you?

_____

_____

_____

What health issues do you have at the moment?

_____

_____

_____

What do you think a new job could help with?

_____

_____

_____

What is it about this organisation that is hindering your health?

_____

_____

_____

What is it about this situation that is hindering your health?

___

What do you want to be doing?

___

How do you want to feel?

___

In an ideal day what would your routine look like so that health comes first?

___

Culture – it's a club I'm not part of

Nobody deserves to be in a job they dislike. Nobody deserves to work for a manager who doesn't respect them.

Are you looking for a workplace that is a better match to your dreams, desires, and values? Do you think that there must be something more to life, that a better balance must be out there? That you'd like to try at least?

Is your manager kind, caring, trustworthy and progressive? Or are they stuck in the past, not wanting to change? What do you think of the way they speak to you or others? Are they motivational or dictatorial?

Do you want an organisation that is adaptable and willing to change? One that listens and responds to people? Are you worried about poor behaviours and toxic leaders? What type of culture and environment do you really want to work in?

Sometimes we can just feel like a square peg in a round hole. Sometimes others around us can be toxic. Sometimes the way an organisation wants to be – their mission, values, vision – just doesn't align with our way of doing things.

A study by Robert Walters found that over 70% of people have left an organisation because they disliked the culture.[9] According to the Trust Gap report, over 50% of people have witnessed or experienced workplace bullying and 45% of people have left the organisation as a result.[10]

Finding a good cultural match for your vision and values can make a huge difference to how you feel about work and the type of organisation you want to work for.

If you are anti-smoking, you are unlikely to get on well in a large tobacco company even if you are great at your job. If you are a softly softly salesperson who builds relationships, you are unlikely to be successful in a ruthless, target-driven environment.

Sometimes we like the organisation, but our leader is the toxic one. Perhaps you are finding it impossible to get your point across, or maybe they are taking you for granted, expecting you to work longer

---

9   Professionals report leaving a job due to poor cultural fit, Robert Walters, https://www.robertwalters.ie/news/cultural-fit-research1.html

10   The Trust Gap: Expectation vs Reality in Workplace Misconduct, Vault Platform, https://vaultplatform.com/the-trust-gap/

hours than you can, putting you under pressure or taking credit for your work. According to a Gallup[11] poll, 50% of people quit their job because of a bad leader, not a bad job.

Tick below any of the boxes that apply to you.

CULTURE ☐

BAD LEADER / MANAGER ☐

 **Exercise**

Bad Leader

What is it about the current culture that is misaligned for you?

Some things to consider:

- Mission
- Vision
- Values
- Leadership approach
- Mix of people — all male, for example
- Results at all costs
- Lies / dishonesty
- Inherent racism / discrimination
- Laddish / sexist behaviours
- Bad behaviour / talking down / patronising / overlooked
- No investment / cost cutting / redundancy
- Outsourcing / insourcing
- No fun
- Culture of change which you don't agree with
- Politics

---

11 Employees Want a Lot More From Their Managers, Gallup, https://www.gallup.com/workplace/236570/employees-lot-managers.aspx

Even if you think that by staying you can change some of these cultures, depending on your position and influence it can be an impossible task, an uphill battle. And the question is, do you want to continue to fight that battle? Or do you want to work for a more enlightened organisation that can help you now, be more enjoyable now?

Questions:

What do you identify about the culture that is not working?

___

___

___

What is it specifically?

___

___

___

___

Is there anything that can be changed within?

___

___

___

Can you speak up to change it?

___

___

___

Is it an organisation-wide issue or just local?

_____

_____

_____

What can you identify about the toxic culture that you don't like?

_____

_____

_____

What traits of good culture do you want to be looking for?

_____

_____

_____

_____

Paternity leave / Maternity returner / Planning a family

> 'The Equalities and Human Rights Commission conducted a formal investigation into pregnancy discrimination in 2015. Their final report found that 54,000 women a year are forced out of their job because of pregnancy discrimination, one in five mothers experienced harassment and negative comments because of their pregnancy and 10% of mothers were discouraged from taking time off for their antenatal care.'[12]

Life changes when you have a baby. You think it won't, but it does. Suddenly there are 100 other things to do in your day and the same number of hours. Plus, you are doing it all on less sleep. Unless you are incredibly fortunate and have a full-time nanny, you have to pick up the slack.

My role was made redundant when I was pregnant with my second child. The writing was probably already on the wall because I was one of the first people to be pregnant and take maternity leave. There were a few comments made about being a 'part-timer' and the worst comment I overheard was someone senior saying that they 'didn't pay people to go off and have babies'. Searching for a job when pregnant was tricky but I knew I needed to find a better cultural fit.

Here, the type of organisation can really make a difference. Do they have family-friendly policies and an accepting culture? There are obviously bare minimum legal requirements such as maternity and adoption leave, parental leave, and emergency care for dependants, but what else do they offer?

Some organisations offer paid childcare, on-site nurseries, fertility leave, enhanced maternity leave, paid leave for fathers, emergency childcare cover and annualised contract hours.[13]

If you had a baby or undertook an adoption during lockdown and your maternity leave is coming to an end, you might be considering, is your organisation the right match for what your priorities are right now?

---

12   Pregnancy discrimination, Maternity Action, https://maternityaction.org.uk/advice/pregnancy-discrimination/

13   Family-friendly leave policies are key to staff retention, Financial Times, 5 December 2021, https://www.ft.com/content/b14b4e7a-e87d-4aee-a267-8100661e4b57

You might be one of many parents who are making the transition from nursery to primary school, or to secondary school and the new routines that it brings, and you want to be home for them, doing the school run.

You might have teenage children who are having mental health issues, who are struggling to get back into the world themselves. They might need you now more than ever.

Just as women want to work, men want to parent. Men want to make choices about flexible working, remote working and taking time off with their newborn baby. And why shouldn't they. Flexible working is often discussed as if it is a women-only issue. Articles and conferences, adverts and workshops are pitched at women. However, men want this flexibility too.

Men want to spend time with their kids; they want to support their partners. Their partners may be the main earner in the house, and they are OK with that. They might take shared parental leave. They want to take their holidays and want to work in an organisation where there is a culture that supports these requirements.

For men, stress is still a major issue and there is still a stigma about talking about it. Suicide is still the highest killer of men aged 25–40 in the UK. Men are 3.5 times more likely to die from suicide than women according to a WHO study.[14] If men are still pressured to work the standard 9–5 working pattern, not take their holiday, not take parental leave, then we are potentially seeing a generation of men who are choosing what they SHOULD be doing over what they WANT to be doing.[15]

Are you a man wanting to work for an organisation that supports your future family set-up? Where taking paternity leave is not seen as a weakness? Where finishing on time to collect children is accepted as the norm?[16]

If this area is a key driver then tick the box.

PATERNITY / MATERNITY / FAMILY POLICIES ☐

---

14   Why more men than women die by suicide, BBC Future, 18 March 2019, https://www.bbc.com/future/article/20190313-why-more-men-kill-themselves-than-women

15   Number of fathers taking paternity leave plunges to '10-year low', The Independent, 23 August 2021, https://www.independent.co.uk/news/uk/home-news/paternity-leave-fathers-10-year-low-b1906074.html

16   'It was seen as weird': why are so few men taking shared parental leave?, Family, The Guardian, 5 October 2019, https://www.theguardian.com/lifeandstyle/2019/oct/05/shared-parental-leave-seen-as-weird-paternity-leave-in-decline

 # Exercise

Paternity / Maternity / Family Policies

What would you like from an employer when thinking about family policies?

_____
_____
_____

What examples of good policies have you seen that are appealing? Or essential?

_____
_____
_____

What big milestones are coming up in the next few years that might influence your decision now? (e.g. nursery transition, another child, adoption, GCSE years)

_____
_____
_____
_____

Caring responsibilities

According to Carers UK, 1.8 million workers took on additional caring responsibilities when the pandemic began.[17] Responses were good at the start of the pandemic, with 9 out of 10 employers surveyed providing extra support, flexibility, or additional leave for those supporting family members. But one year later a survey of carers showed that 62% were worried that the temporary support might be withdrawn as working patterns returned to 'normal'.

Do you have caring responsibilities that need to be factored into your job search?

Women are reported to be leaving the workplace after the pandemic, as they shoulder the largest proportion of the caring burden. Perhaps you are thinking of leaving the work environment because you don't see a good fit for the way you'd like to be working. If your life and caring arrangements have changed then it is likely that the work you do, or where you do it, might need to change with it.

Elderly relatives or family members might be needing more support now and you want to be there to give it to them.

A staggering 3.2m people got a pet during the pandemic.[18] Were you one of them? Having a pet changes your routine and your lifestyle — which you may need to now factor into any search.

If caring responsibilities have become a factor in your search, then tick below.

CARING RESPONSIBILITIES ☐

---

[17] Supporting working carers in COVID-19, employer survey, Carers UK, https://www.carersuk.org/images/Research/CUK_State_of_Caring_2021_report_web.pdf

[18] Households 'buy 3.2 million pets in lockdown', BBC News, 12 March 2021, https://www.bbc.co.uk/news/business-56362987

 **Exercise**

Caring

What has changed since the pandemic?

_____
_____
_____

What are your caring responsibilities now?

_____
_____
_____

What impact does that have on your search?

_____
_____
_____

What will you need from your new role?

_____
_____
_____

Redundancy or Settlement Agreement

Restructures and redundancies are commonplace nowadays. Maybe you are one of those who lost their job during the highest peak of redundancy ever seen? You may have been in a job you loved, with a culture that you felt a real affinity to.

> 'The ONS's labour market overview for January 2021 shows that the aggregate redundancy rate increased to a record high of 14.2 per thousand employees between July and November 2020. The redundancy rate for men (15.5 per thousand) was higher than that for women (12.8 per thousand).'[19]

You might have been someone on the receiving end of a Settlement Agreement, without the formal redundancy process, sometimes known as the 'tap on the shoulder' with an NDA (Non-Disclosure Agreement).

Redundancy is stressful and can be a huge shock. It's happened to me twice. Once out of the blue, and once I was part of the decision-making process and knew it was coming along. Whether you know it is coming or not it can be disruptive, scary, disorientating and worrying.

> *I realised once I had taken redundancy that a lot of my status and how I labelled myself was to do with work. Once that job title and company wasn't there anymore, I felt a bit bereft and lost. I had to rethink who I was and what I stood for without the back-up of a large well-known company name behind me.*

Later we will look at how you can cope with the stress of your role being made redundant and how to get your confidence back, but for now, if this is your reason for being here, tick the box.

REDUNDANCY ☐

---

[19] Labour market overview, UK, Office for National Statistics, https://www.ons.gov.uk/employmentandlabourmarket/peopleinwork/employmentandemployeetypes/bulletins/uklabourmarket/january2021

 # Exercise

Redundancy

How do you feel about the redundancy?

___

What would you keep about the old role / organisation?

___

What would you change?

___

What sort of organisation do you want to work for now?

___

Money saving

You've got used to not spending money on the commute, the daily coffee and sandwich. You prefer saving. With inflation levels rising you may be looking to reduce your external expenditure related to work.

> 'Last year, in total, households put away almost three times as much money as the year before, according to an analysis of Bank of England figures by the investment firm Hargreaves Lansdown. It found that in the year to March 2021, £184bn flowed into savings accounts.'[20]

MONEY SAVING ☐

✏ Exercise

Money Saving

What have you not been spending money on?

_____

_____

_____

How much do you think you are saving?

_____

_____

---

20 Coronavirus: impact on household debt and savings, Brigid Francis-Devine, 6 July 2021, House of Commons Library, https://researchbriefings.files.parliament.uk/documents/CBP-9060/CBP-9060.pdf

What does saving this money mean for you and your family?

_____

_____

_____

What does this mean for your search?

_____

_____

_____

What other reasons are driving your search? What else are you thinking about that I have not mentioned here?

_____

_____

_____

Make a note of anything else that is coming to mind.

_____

_____

_____

_____

Checkpoint – Look before you leap!

It is important to recognise that the grass is not always greener on the other side!

 **Case Study**

Fergus

Do you always need to leave to get what you want?

The grass is not always greener so reviewing where you are at is a valuable exercise to do.

Fergus approached me for coaching support because he wanted more of a challenge in his role. He was thinking of leaving but wasn't sure because he loved the organisation.

We started by looking at what was frustrating him.

He wanted more challenge; he wanted opportunities to be more proactive. He wanted to be more creative. He'd loved getting involved in a Black Lives Matter mentoring scheme. He wanted to be learning more. He didn't really want to leave but felt it might be his only option.

Having discovered where he was 'lacking' in life, we then explored other inventive ways of achieving that goal without necessarily leaving.

He realised that he could choose to be more proactive and do more volunteering within the Black Lives Matter campaign. He could push himself forward, learn more and help others. It would be a challenge.

He realised that he could take part in more of the local and regional events that were available, to help expand his network and help him to keep learning.

He realised that now was the time to study for a qualification that had interested him, which up to now he hadn't had the time to do.

He realised that one of his favourite hobbies, songwriting, was very creative. He could be proactive and take more time outside of work to pursue that, fulfilling his creative urge.

He concluded that the job itself was interesting and varied. The organisation culture was good. They were trying to improve in areas like diversity and he could take an active role in that cultural change, which was inspiring to him.

He concluded that now was not the time to leave.

Take some time to think about whether there is anything you CAN do in your current role to make it work for you?

_____

_____

_____

Are there any actions that you can take to make your current role more palatable?

_____

_____

_____

Could you have a conversation with your line manager / HR?

_____

_____

_____

Is there any support available such as via an Employee Assistance Programme (EAP)?

_____

_____

_____

Could you take action yourself and delegate / remove work?

_____

_____

_____

Go back through the list of key drivers and make a note here of all the boxes you ticked. Take some time to consider the questions in those sections. Are there any other reasons, not mentioned, that resonate for you? Make a note of those as well. Don't worry if you need to come back to it over a number of days; there are a lot of questions! Taking stock and identifying your reasons for moving can be incredibly informative as we move through the book.

Now review the list and prioritise it. Note down the main driver for change and then number each other driver by order of priority.

Main driver: _____

Other priorities in order:

1. _____

2. _____

3. _____

4. _____

5. _____

6. _____

What does this tell you about where your search should be focussed?

_____

_____

_____

Make any other notes so you can refer back as we build your **ideal job checklist**.

_____

_____

_____

 **Summary**

1. Review all of the potential reasons for your job search

2. Identify your key drivers

3. Make a note of the main reasons for moving role now

Chapter 4

Who are you?

Happiness at work

YOU SPEND SO much of your life at work that you deserve to be happy when you are there, right? So many people I meet and speak to think that 'work is work'; they often shrug and say, 'It is what it is' or 'I have no choice'.

But the thing is we all have a CHOICE and so do YOU.

There is another way. You can choose to look for work that is better than the work you have today. It might not be perfect, but it can be *better*. The trick is knowing who you are and what it is about your thoughts and feelings that mean you want to look for something different right now.

In this section we are going to be doing a number of exercises that will help you to understand what makes you tick, what makes you the person you are. Exploring our own personal beliefs, purpose and ethos can help us to understand why we might be a better fit in one organisation than another.

Take your time with the exercises. I'd encourage you not to rush at this stage, as the information will be an important building block for the conclusions you make later on. If need be, have a break, make a cuppa and come back and do the next step later.

What choices are you making?

To make good choices you need to know:

1. What are your values — your deep core beliefs that act like a compass for you and everything you do?

If you strongly believe in honesty and trust, you won't suit working for a cut-throat manager who wants to cut corners, to have 'success at any cost'.

2. What makes you happy — what truly makes your heart sing, what gives you a buzz, what makes you content? Not just in work but in life.

If you love spending time with your family, then 10 hours a week on a train will just depress you.

3. What do you want in a job — what are you trying to achieve? Are you simply trying to pay the bills, steadily and with no fuss, or are you looking for promotion and opportunity? Are you wanting to develop new skills, learn a little, go into a new field, travel the world, meet new friends or be part of a community?

If you have career aspirations, then a steady organisation might not give you the opportunities you seek.

4. What is your purpose — finding out what you are trying to achieve is a tricky question. Your purpose might have nothing to do with work; your purpose might be to bring up your children well, be part of a larger community, give back to the environment, do charity fundraising. Your job might be a means to an end, so how much time and effort will you give to it?

If you could you do a job that is aligned to your purpose so that you feel like you are meeting that purpose in all areas of your life, would that feel better?

5. What does your job bring you? This isn't just about earning money — although that is ultimately what we are there for. Are you looking for more status, more earnings or are you looking for connections, satisfaction, making a difference to people's lives, maybe changing the world? What benefits do you gain by being part of the organisation? You might covet a huge discount, or you might get a sense of pride from working in the charity sector, or the benefits package might be very helpful to you and your family — for example healthcare.

If you want to make a difference, then the values of the organisation you work for will be of huge importance.

6. What is your direction — this might depend on where you are in your career or your life. And things change all the time. What is the direction you want to be travelling in right now? Are you on an upwards trajectory — all rocket ships blazing, aiming to get to the top as quickly as possible? Or are you looking for a holding pattern right now where work can take a back seat while you focus on health or family? Maybe you are looking to take a side turn to a new sector or learn a new skill?

If you are focussing on health and family, then an organisation with child-friendly policies and flexibility might be more appealing.

What YOU want will be different to what others want. If you know what you want, you can be much more focussed in your search. You'll be happier in the role you get.

Case Study

Neal

This story shows the importance of knowing your values.

My husband was in a large professional firm, on track to be a partner after coming top in his year in his accountancy exams.

Then we had a baby. All bets were off. Everything changed.

He noticed that his line manager, the partner, often called home at 7pm from the office to say 'goodnight' to his children. He thought 'I don't want to be like that'.

He noticed that his colleagues were often going drinking after late night working, rather than catching the train home to their families. He thought 'I don't want to be like that'.

He noticed that other colleagues were embarking on affairs, because they weren't part of family life and were getting sucked into the corporate after-party life. He thought 'I don't want to be like that'.

He was getting up before our daughter woke up and coming home after she had gone to sleep. He was missing a lot of her early months. He thought 'I don't want life to be like this'.

He wanted to have a strong relationship with his family and to have his children know him. Not to wake up in 15 years' time and realise that he had no relationship with them. He knew he had to make a change.

His values of family, our marriage, his long-term relationship with his children were all so important to him that he looked for a job much closer to home. It was less money, less prospects, less prestige. But it meant he got to say good morning to his children, and to take part in bath time routines.

That was a key decision for him and ultimately it led him on a different path. He is now the owner of several different businesses and has achieved business success in a different way than the initial path laid out for him early on. He is still married. He has wonderful relationships with his children. He wanted it to be like that.

 **Exercise**

Values

Sometimes we know we want to work somewhere with a different culture, but we are not sure what that means, what it looks like or why that is the case.

By looking at your own core values you can start to explore what is important to you.

This can be a really good way of finding a good match of culture and the type of people you want to work with later, when you are ready to explore the market.

Some organisations may ask you what your values are, and how you see yourself fitting into their culture. So, it is worth knowing what yours are — for many reasons!

Work through the Values Exercise sheets on the next few pages and take some time to go through them. It will take approximately 20–25 minutes. Make sure you leave some time to reflect on what the answers tell you about the sort of organisation you might want to work with in the future. Make notes and write down any thoughts that come up for you.

Values Exercise

Take a look at all of these words listed below: Take a pen and circle the 20 (or so) words that resonate with you the most:

Big picture	Financial security	Compassion
Health/Fitness	Nature	Accomplishment
Dependability	Loyalty	Beauty
Bravery	Safety	Gratitude
Love	Connection	Relationships
Learning	Leadership	Survival
Achievement	Self-Preservation security	Adventure
Family	Hard work	Results
Spontaneity	Success	Boldness
Calm	Freedom	Fun
Happiness	Wealth	Strategy
Decision making	Dreams	Helping society
Creative	Wellbeing	Respect
Quality of life	Recognition	Spirituality
Art	Challenge	Change
Clarity	Humour	Harmony
Experimentation	Excitement	Standing up for good
Peace	Passion	Curiosity
Equality	Justice	Forgiveness
Trust	Growth	Speaking up
Honesty	Imagination	Innovation
Inspiration	Laughter	Making a difference
Optimism	Perspective	Determination
Play	Power	Professional
Integrity	Quietness	Stability
Respect	Taking risks	Tolerance
Understanding	Wonder	Choice
Luxury	Freedom	Time alone
Story telling	Fairness	Forgiveness
Contentment	World views	Collaboration
Generosity	Journey	Co-operation

Now take some time to review the ones you have circled.

What do you notice?

Are there any common themes? Group those together.

Remove any now that do not resonate on a second look.

Now — choose your top 6 values.

1. _____

2. _____

3. _____

4. _____

5. _____

6. _____

Now you have identified your top 6 values, you can take some time to assess how well you are living and breathing them in different aspects of your life.

Consider relationships, family, home life, work, health and fitness, hobbies and pastimes.

As you review each of your top 6, make any notes about how well things are going. What might you change?

1. _____

2. _____

3. _____

4. _____

5. _____

6. _____

Take some time to explore what might need to change. How might your work be making an impact?

_____

_____

_____

Are there any immediate thoughts as to what you might want to do differently?

_____

_____

_____

Are there any actions or thoughts you would like to note down?

_____

_____

_____

Are there any observations that come up that are particular to your dream job, culture or career that you'd like to note?

_____

_____

_____

_____

PAUSE POINT

Now you have done the Values Exercise, what do you notice?

What has come up?

_____

_____

How do your top values impact on the sort of role you are looking for?

_____

_____

What does the Values Exercise tell you about your deep-rooted ideals and core beliefs as they relate to work?

_____

_____

_____

 **Exercise**

Choices

What makes you happy?

What makes you happy — what truly makes your heart sing, what gives you a buzz, what makes you content? Not just in work but in life.

Write down the things that make you happy:

___

___

___

___

___

___

___

___

___

___

What do you want to achieve / What is your purpose?

What is your purpose? What is your overall aim in life right now?

_____

_____

_____

What do you want in a job — what are you trying to achieve?

_____

_____

_____

What do you love to do and want to do more of?

_____

_____

_____

What do you deep down want to be doing with your life overall?

_____

_____

_____

What does work bring you? / What outcomes do you get from working?

What does work bring you?

_____

_____

_____

What are you looking for from your work or career?

_____

_____

_____

What benefits do you gain by being part of the organisation?

_____

_____

_____

What are you looking for work to achieve?

_____

_____

_____

What direction are you travelling in right now?

What is your direction right now? Your direction right now will be different to 2 years ago, and different to what it might be in 9 months' time.

___

___

___

___

___

___

___

What is affecting your direction of travel right now?

___

___

___

Make a note of where your current direction is leading you:

___

___

___

___

 **Summary**

Make sure you have:

1. Completed the 'Choices' Exercise

2. Completed the 'Values' Exercise

3. Considered what makes you happy

4. Reflected on your direction of travel right now

Chapter 5

Digging deeper

IN THE LAST chapter you started to explore who you are, what your values are, and you started to note down where you are currently at, reflecting on a number of different aspects of your life, direction and purpose. In this section you will start to look a little deeper into some of the cultural aspects of work, and how they influence the choices you might make for your next role.

Life is a page

If our life is a page, how much of it is written on by work? How long do we live and how many years are we at work?

Let's keep the maths easy and say we start work at 20 and retire at 60. That is 40 years of our life. If we live until we are 80 that is half of our life. If our life is a page, half of it is at work.

Do you keep clear boundaries between home and work? Is work so pleasurable that you don't mind when you work? Or is work eating into your home life? As you are reading this book, I suspect that there is something you'd like to change. You want to be sure that you are working on something you love and with people you like, if this is half of your life!

But if only it was as easy to compartmentalise — 'work' on one side and 'life' on the other.

To start with you might think, well, I work a 40-hour week, so that is about a quarter of the week.[21] Not bad at first glance. A quarter of the page for work. Is the work section of the page in a nice clean box — where the writing doesn't infiltrate the rest of the page? Or is work all over your page of life?

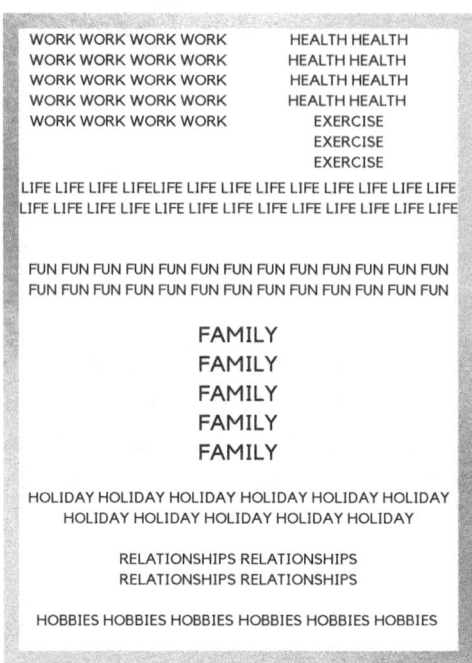

If Your Life is a Page...

What about the times when you are checking emails after hours, or first thing in the morning? When you wake up in the night with a 'to-do' list in your head, or when your brain starts rehearsing conversations? When you talk about work with your partner or friends? When you moan about your management to anyone who will listen? What about the commute time? What about on a Sunday night when you just log in to 'check and prep' your week — how many hours is that?

How much scrawl just went all over your 'life' page?

---

21   168 divided by 40 hours (24 hours x 7 days)

If Your Life is a Page...

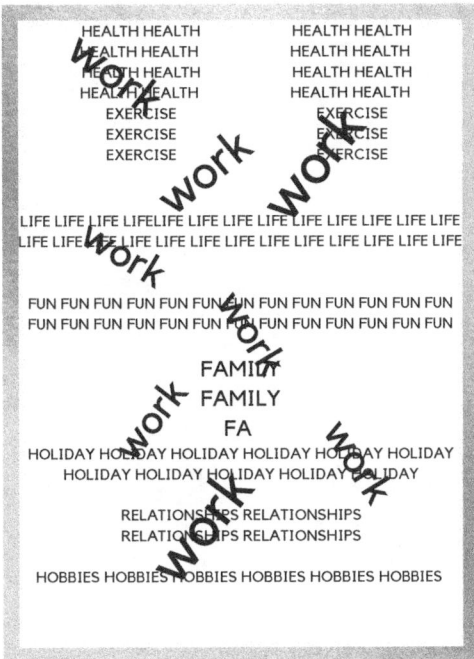

If you love your work, then you don't mind if work becomes part of your life. If you don't love work or the culture is not a great fit, then it can cause stress, resentment, and worry.

I wonder how your page looks?

Make a note of what your 'page' looks like.

If Your Life is a Page...

Is work in a neat and tidy box? Or is work writing all over your page? How many hours of work are infiltrating into your everyday life?

Think about your life right now — not what it might be in the future; think about the current influences, obligations and requirements on your time.

What else do you notice from this exercise?

_____

_____

_____

_____

A coaching client spoke to me about wanting promotion and his opening line was 'I think I should be a senior manager by now'. We explored what his page looked like at the moment, looking at the external factors that were influencing his life such as his health and the fact that he was now the father of a young baby. I asked him, 'Instead of thinking about where you think you SHOULD be, let's think about what you WANT your page to look like right now?' After some thought he said, 'I want to be a present father for my son, I want to improve my health. Actually, I want to be a football coach and have time for that rather than working all the hours.' Taking a step back, he could see that the SHOULD had come from a lifetime of familial pressure and expectation. It was time for him to make choices based on his own time of life right now!

Consider whether you might share this reflection with your partner or family member. You might discuss your findings with them. Do they think the same as you about how work and life are balanced across your page of life?

Culture

How do you know when the culture is right?

You know almost instinctively when it is wrong!

When we are looking for a new role, it is not as simple as just finding a new job description and the right salary. This time you want to find a job that also *feels* right. Where you feel like you fit in, where you are making a difference, where you feel comfortable, where you are recognised, rewarded, where you are enjoying your days and not counting down the minutes until 5pm.

Signs that a culture is wrong for you:

Physical signs

- Feeling stressed
- Headaches
- Sweaty palms
- Sick feeling / nausea
- Recurring illnesses restart
- Nervous tics — shaking / fidgets
- Stop sleeping / Waking in the night
- Oversleeping / Lethargic

Mental and emotional signs

- Anxiety
- Depression
- Constant worry
- Tearful
- Fearful
- Angry

Behavioural signs

- Overeating / undereating
- Avoidance of work
- Avoidance of social life / things you used to enjoy
- Quiet / reclusive
- Drinking too much to forget / relax
- Overwork

 **Exercise**

How I Want to Feel

Think about how you *WANT* to feel at work. Write down how you would feel if you were in a role you loved, with an organisation that you respected, and they respected you.

Physically I would feel:

e.g. free of headaches, well, relaxed

_____

_____

Mentally and emotionally, I would feel:

e.g. calm, happy, content

_____

_____

Behaviourally I would feel:

e.g. better able to sleep and would have some energy to exercise

_____

_____

 **Exercise**

Negative Culture

How do you know what a 'wrong' culture looks like for you? Have a look at the list and see what you can recognise from your current role or from past roles. What things in particular are triggers for you, or things you really want to avoid? Make a note of them or mark them as you go through the list.

What a negative culture can be like:

Leadership

- Bullying
- Harassment
- Taking the credit for work of others
- No praise or recognition
- Overly high expectations
- No work-life balance
- Culture of work hard play hard (when you don't want that)
- Not listening to opinions of staff
- Not asking for opinions from staff
- Ignoring reports of issues
- Underpaying
- Not recognising talent
- Favouritism
- Discriminatory behaviours – covert or overt

Structure

- Oppression of views
- No autonomy
- Presentism culture (rather than focus on productive work)
- Overly authoritarian
- Double checking of work
- Clock watching
- No freedom to express opinions or views

Atmosphere

- Gossip
- Backbiting
- Cliques
- No formal routes of communication
- Hearsay
- Tale-telling
- Act now think later
- Overly direct
- No compassion

Team

- Overly competitive
- Wrong people recognised for work
- Errors hidden or not acknowledged
- Customers ignored or not treated well
- No team building or investment
- Avoiding speaking up when you know the culture is wrong
- Fear of getting it wrong

Signs of a good culture — what you can learn before you start!

It can be helpful to know what we want in a culture before we get to a place of work, but how can we find out before we get there?

If work-life balance is key for you then keeping an eye out for LinkedIn articles and press statements from the organisation you are looking to join can be helpful. What have the leaders said recently about the way they want people to work?

The Goldman Sachs Chairman said that *'remote working was an aberration that needed to be stopped as soon as possible'*[22]. Apple announced that they wanted people in the office for 3 days a week[23]. Salesforce said that *'9–5 was dead'*[24] and Deloitte declared that people could work *'wherever they wanted'*[25]. Policies are changing all the time, and the various divisions of organisations will have differing opinions depending on the role.

Looking at the latest articles published by an organisation might give you a sign as to the sort of tone and expectation that they might put on their staff.

Make a note of any organisations you already know have a good culture that you are keen to explore:

---

[22] Goldman Sachs: Bank boss rejects work from home as the 'new normal', BBC News, 25 Feb 2021, https://www.bbc.co.uk/news/business-56192048

[23] Apple wants staff back in offices by September, BBC News, 3 June 2021, https://www.bbc.co.uk/news/technology-57342768

[24] Creating a Best Workplace from Anywhere, for Everyone, Salesforce News, https://www.salesforce.com/news/stories/creating-a-best-workplace-from-anywhere/

[25] Deloitte gives its 20,000 people the choice of when and where they work, Deloitte UK, https://www2.deloitte.com/uk/en/pages/press-releases/articles/deloitte-gives-its-20000-people-the-choice-of-when-and-where-they-work.html

 Exercise

Positive Culture

Use the list below to identify the key points you are looking for from a good culture.

What a positive culture can be like:

Leadership

- Supportive
- Inclusive
- Acknowledging the efforts of the whole team
- Outward praise, reward and recognition tools in place and utilised
- Realistic expectations – an understanding of the issues and the market
- Flexible approach to work-life balance
- Responsive to opinions of staff
- Regularly asking for opinions from staff
- Taking action on reports of issues
- Paying fair market rate – or better
- Recognising talent and having succession planning in place
- Fair behaviour for all
- Not tolerating any discriminatory behaviour, active in stamping it out
- Communications are clear

Structure

- Openly asking for views and taking actions from all levels
- Giving freedom, autonomy and responsibility to all
- Flexible approach to working patterns, productive behaviour rewarded over presentism
- Flat structures
- Checks and measures and trust
- Time management freedom
- Asking for opinions and creativity from people
- Actively encouraging change
- Actively rewarding creativity

Atmosphere

- Friendly, fair
- Open and clear
- We are all part of a team
- Communications, clear, concise, regular and to all
- Feedback encouraged and listened to

Chapter 5: Digging deeper

- Planning / organisation / considered approach
- Consultative

- Compassionate
- Supportive
- Confidence boosting

Team

- Competitive as a group, for the organisation
- Right people recognised for work
- Errors openly discussed and improvements noted and encouraged
- Customers treated well

- Investment in people, training, development
- Hiring the right people at the right time
- People feel comfortable speaking up
- Whistle blowing processes in place
- Employee support programmes in place
- People are consulted and informed

Looking at the lists, and what you have noted against both the positive and negative culture exercises, what can you learn about the type of organisation you want to work for in the future? What signs are you going to be looking for as you do your research? Make a note for your **ideal job checklist**.

_____

_____

_____

You can come back to this section over the next few days and weeks, adding anything new that you notice about the culture at your current work, or when you remember something. It can be useful to keep adding to your lists so that you have it to refer back to.

Ethos and approach

How you work is more than just your set of skills and the values you hold. You have a *way* of working too. It's just how you do things. Your work ethic, your ethos, is heavily aligned to your values. Let's explore a little deeper here to understand how your ethos steers how you work. This can tell you more about how you want to work and the sort of organisation you want to be part of in the future.

How do I know what my ethos is?

It can be helpful to start by looking at common phrases we often use in our work. We will all have them. They give others a kind of shorthand as to who we are and how we do things. They can also sometimes hide bad behaviours, traits, and excuses we make.

Here are a few I have come across — do you recognise any that sum up how you work yourself? If so, make a note or mark against them:

- I don't suffer fools
- The customer is always right
- The customer is not always right
- Measure twice, cut once
- You can't manage what you don't measure
- We win as a team
- My door is always open
- I don't abide gossip — straight talking only
- Stick to the facts
- Planning is key
- The best ideas are the simplest ideas
- No question is a silly question
- No surprises
- One thing at a time
- Everything is an opportunity
- Everyone is a salesperson
- Hire for talent, train for skill
- Progress not perfection
- Bring the fun back
- No-one is indispensable
- Firm but fair
- Evolution not revolution

- Any decision is better than no decision
- A change is as good as a rest
- Stability is key
- Just do it
- Time waits for no-one
- Don't stagnate — innovate!
- Nothing changes if nothing changes
- The grass isn't always greener
- To fail to prepare is to prepare to fail
- Slow and steady wins the race
- It is what it is

What are your stock phrases? Are there some statements you always use? Some mantras that you state whenever you join a new team?

_____

_____

_____

These will give you a clue as to the sort of values you have. Do they tie together with your values?

Can you see which are more positive in slant than negative?

Are there statements that are totally aligned with the person you want to be and the job you want and the culture of the business you want to work at?

_____

_____

_____

_____

Perhaps you always introduce yourself as a certain type of leader? A type of worker?

Make a note of anything that comes to mind.

_____
_____
_____
_____
_____
_____
_____
_____
_____
_____

Understanding ourselves and how we want to work can be very valuable when we are looking for a matching culture and a similar energy. If an organisation talks about 'time waits for no-one' and you are more of a 'slow and steady wins the race' person then there might be a clash of ethos and approach. Clashes can (not always) be a cause of tension and stress, so understanding your own ethos can mean that you start looking out for likeminded organisations.

 Summary

Now you have completed the exercises in this section you will have a better understanding of your values and your ethos.

Make sure you have:

1. **Completed the 'Life is a Page' Exercise**
2. **Completed the 'How I Want to Feel' Exercise**
3. **Considered the 'Culture' Exercises**
4. **Reflected on your own ethos**

Now as we move to the next chapter, we can start to identify more details about the job you really want.

Chapter 6

Designing your dream job – what do you want?

WHEN I STARTED looking for work as a student, I gave zero thought to the type of organisation or business I wanted to work in. I looked for something in my area, paying a reasonable salary and, frankly, with an organisation who might accept me with not much experience. I ended up in customer services and the electricity industry and I did well there. It was more luck than judgement at the time. When I look back, though, I had very few criteria on my **ideal job checklist** and so could adapt more easily then. Later, when I had children, my criteria and my **ideal job checklist** got longer and I had many more things I needed from an employer, much more to balance.

What are the things that you want to be doing in your life? What things are starting to formulate that you want to include in your **ideal job checklist**?

The phrase work-life balance starts with 'work' at the front. What about thinking of **life**-work balance? Where life comes first, and work comes second?

Sometimes if work is too much of a priority we can start to think of our work as being on a bit of a hamster wheel that we just want to get off when things are not going well! This is because sometimes we are so out of balance with what we are doing, that work can sometimes take over our whole life. When this happens, we just want to get off the hamster wheel and stop.

I know that when I was feeling completely overwhelmed or suffering with my migraines my default position on a bad day was to say, 'I think I'll just resign'. This statement was my attempt at trying to get a better balance, but it was a kneejerk reaction rather than a planned action.

Instead of stopping completely, take some time to reflect.

This Slice of Life exercise encourages you to reflect and score the different aspects of areas of your life. Be honest — make a note of what is really going on and then you can see what areas are lacking or needing attention. Once it's complete, you can start to see what you might want to correct or change and specifically you can start to see where work fits in and what your criteria and ideal job checklist for new work might be.

Exercise

Slice of Life

This is time to reflect on what your life looks like now and then, more importantly, what you want it to look like in the future.

It can help you to decide how much of your life you want to give to work, family and other aspects of your life, such as hobbies and health.

How much of your life are you spending doing what you really want to be doing? How many slices of your life are given to things like commuting, a job you dislike, or on parts of the job you can do without?

What would you really like a slice of?

Think of your life like a giant cake. You have 168 hours in a week. That is a big cake. What slices are you taking for yourself? Your job? Sleep? Others? Here's an example, and then there's a blank template for you to do your own.

If I work a 40-hour week, sleep 7 hours a night, commute 2 hours a day and watch TV for 3 hours a night it might look like this.

GET THE JOB YOU REALLY WANT

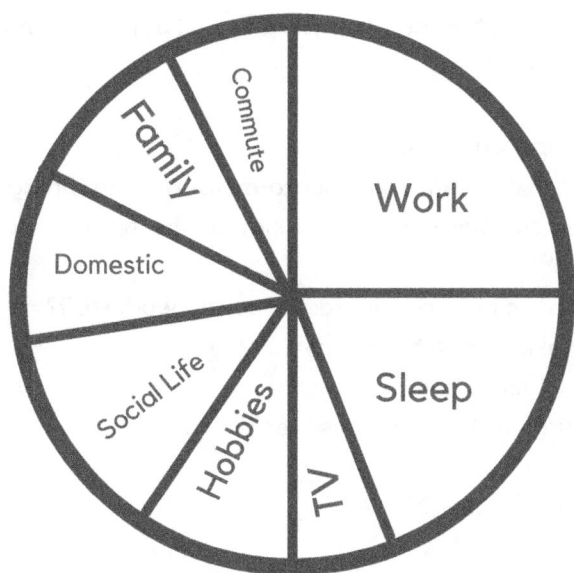

If I work a 70-hour week, sleep 5 hours a night, commute 2 hours a day, work at the weekend for 6 hours, work over breakfast and check my emails before bed it might look like this...

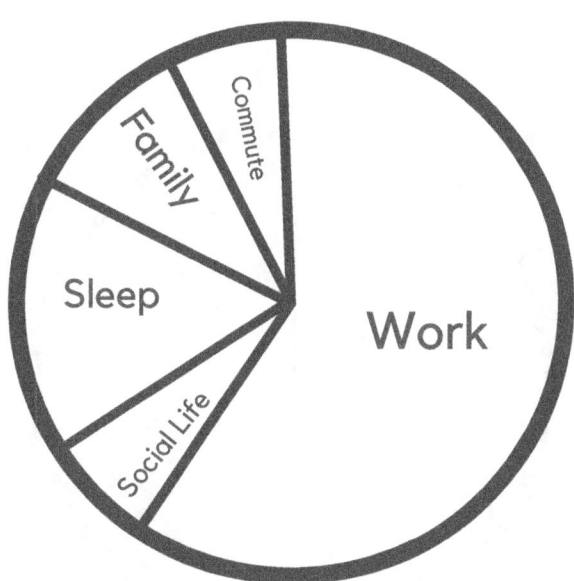

Chapter 6: Designing your dream job — what do you want?

Alternatively, it could look very different if you were to look at how much work is absorbed into your daily life.

- Do you wake up worrying about work?
- Do you get up in the night with your to-do list running through your head?
- Do you spend Sunday night preparing for the return — looking at emails and your calendar?
- Do you spend time before breakfast checking work stuff?
- Do you ever take a lunch break anyway?
- Do you finish on time?
- Do you take urgent calls at the weekend?

What would the example look like then?

Write down how your current life looks. What proportion of time is being given to the various sections?

Your Slice of Life
Current Role / Position

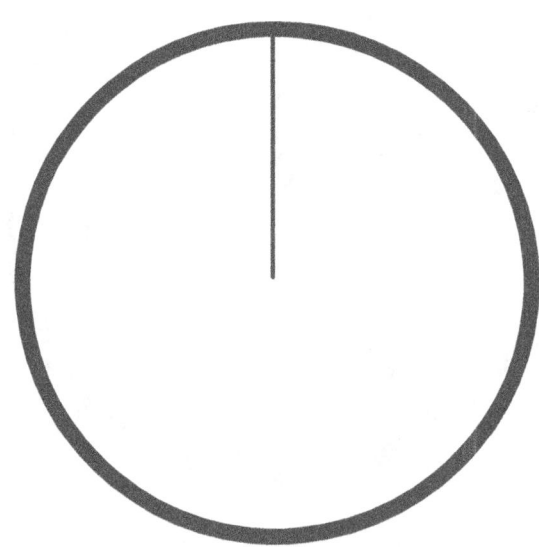

Some areas for you to consider are:

Work / Commute / TV / Internet surfing (be honest!) / Sleep / Family / Gym / Friends and socialising / Hobbies / Domestic tasks (cooking / caring (children / elders) / cleaning etc) / Domestic admin (bills / forms etc) / Any others?

Now is the time to start thinking about the life you really want! Think about what you REALLY want things to look like, in an ideal world. It can help you later when you start to compile your **ideal job checklist**.

Draw what you want your future life to look like. What proportion of time do you want to be giving to the various areas now? What are you going to be doing in your new life?

Your Slice of Life
Future Self - The ideal

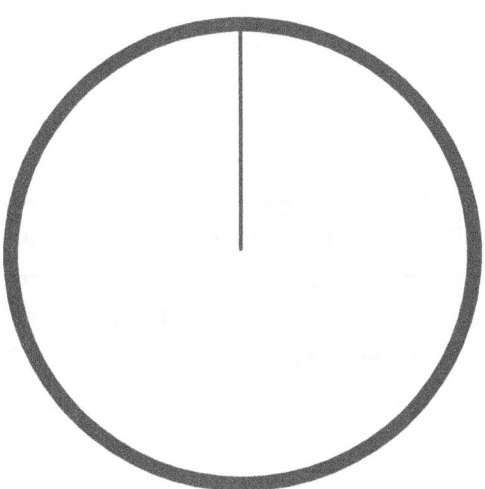

How much time is work taking up now?

Chapter 6: Designing your dream job — what do you want?

Some areas for you to consider are:

Work / Commute / TV / Internet surfing (be honest!) / Sleep / Family / Gym / Friends and socialising / Hobbies / Domestic tasks (cooking / caring (children / elders) / cleaning etc) / Domestic admin (bills / forms etc) / Any others?

Take a look at what you have created, and really absorb what you are seeing and what you are planning.

If your work life is currently 70 hours a week and eating into family time and weekends, and your future life is 30 hours a week for 4 days, these are big changes.

When you come to start looking for the job you really want, these conclusions matter because there is NO POINT looking for a full-time job or one with a culture of working all hours if you want an alternative way of working.

These conclusions will be part of your **ideal job checklist**. It means that if the job description doesn't meet these criteria, it won't make it onto the 'apply for' list.

This exercise might bring a lot to the surface, and that is OK. When doing this exercise, my coaching clients can sometimes realise quite how much time they have been giving to their work rather than to their families, to their relationships and often to themselves. Try not to dwell on any negative aspects of what you have uncovered here. The important thing is that you have started to notice the difference between what you are doing now and what you want for the future. Take some time to have a break and reflect on what has come up.

 **Exercise**

Feeling the Future

Now you have come up with what the slices might look like, use the blank pages here to start to write a few notes about how this new life will FEEL.

You've noted WHAT you will you be doing. What will it be like?

_____

_____

_____

_____

_____

_____

_____

_____

_____

_____

Now think about WHY you are doing it and WHAT it will MEAN for you, for your family, for your health, your wellbeing.

What do you gain? What can you imagine this feels like?

_____
_____
_____
_____
_____
_____
_____
_____
_____
_____

This is an exercise you can repeat. Keep this. And review it whilst you are applying for new roles. When you are being interviewed or weighing up offers, come back to the Slice of Life and think — is this new job going to give me this set of slices? Or close enough?

You might not get *everything* you desire but if it is close enough and you are happy with your compromises then you can redraw the slices with the new hours you will work and plan what you will now be doing.

Then review in 3 and 6 months; certainly review it before your probation period ends. Is this job meeting up with your new expectations? Did the hours really match? How does it feel?

One coaching client, having done the Slice of Life Exercise, realised that they didn't have any hobbies. They simply didn't have any time for them because work was getting in the way. They changed their ideal job to be one that was 4 days a week or finished earlier so that they could get a better balance in their life.

Dream big

Often, we look at the roles and the salary before we think about what we really want to do!

One of my coaching clients wanted to explore next steps when it became apparent that her employer was not going to maintain a level of flexibility when the lockdown ended. She wanted to explore how she could ensure she found a new organisation with a culture that matched her values.

The very first exercise we did together was to explore what her dream job would be if she had no constraints. Using a blank piece of paper, she wrote down where she wanted to work — in an ideal world. How much travel she wanted to do, what hours she wanted to work. Then we turned to the culture — what sort of workplace was she interested in? What sort of people? What would her leaders be like? After exploring her ideals from numerous angles, we could really start to home in on what sort of organisation she should target. All this was done before we even started to explore her skill set, job titles or salary levels. She now had a set of criteria to set up her online searches in a more targeted way. She agreed to only apply for roles that were at least an 80% match or more on her criteria list.

Later she told me that not only had she saved huge amounts of time on not applying to lots of jobs that weren't a good fit, but she'd landed a great job where she just felt like she fitted in from the start.

 **Exercise**

Dream Job Mind Map

Using this mind map, you will start to explore the key aspects of any role — and work out what you want to be doing in an ideal world.

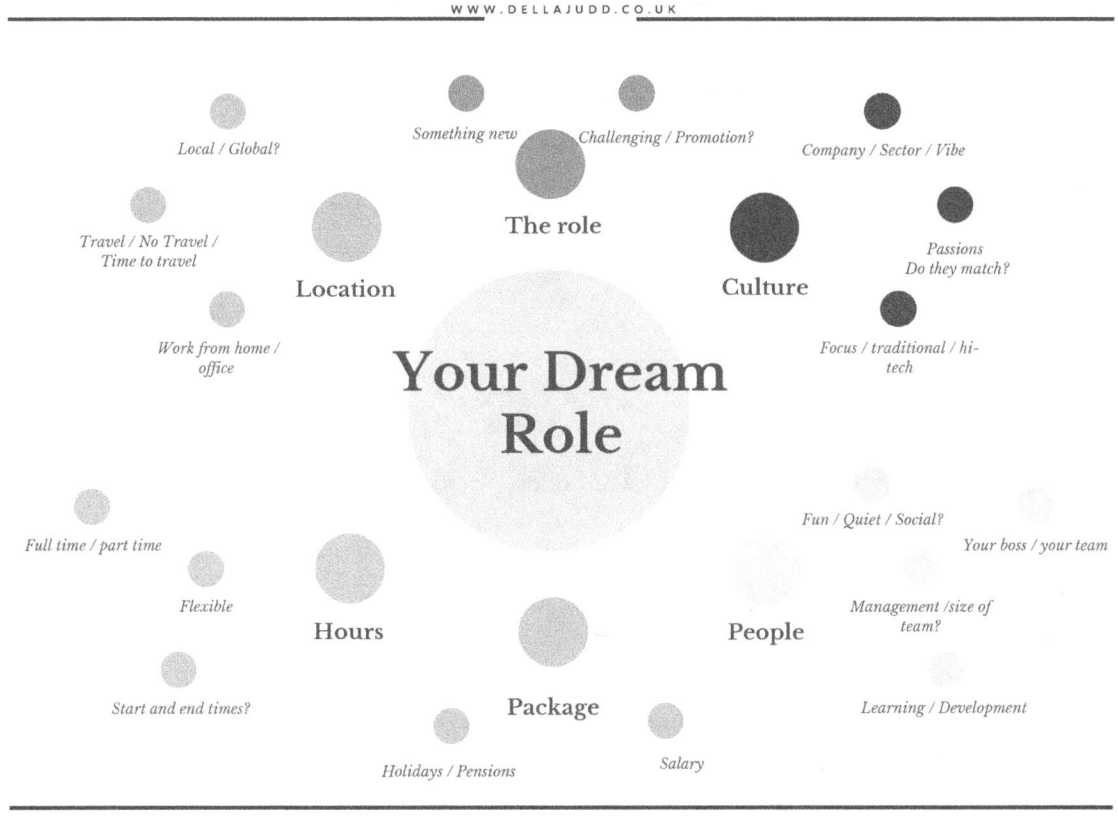

Using a blank piece of paper or the space in the book, use the mind map as a guide to really help you think about what you do and don't want in your next job.

Go through each section and make notes about what you want.

For each area make notes about what comes up.

If you aren't sure, think about what you don't want just as much as what you do want. There can be some useful information there too!

Location:

- Maybe you want to stay local — how local — 5 miles? 10? Walking distance? Or a bus ride?
- Maybe you don't mind occasional travel — weekly, monthly? Is it a trip to London or are we talking long haul?
- Are you now thinking that working from home is ideal? And you don't want to be in the office?
- Do you prefer being in the office and working with others?

_____

_____

_____

Hours:

- Maybe you want to work part time — what does that look like?
- How many hours?
- Which days?
- Flexibility — can you come and go?
- Can you swap shifts?
- Can you take your dentist appointments in a working day?
- Would you like fixed days of the week, or would you prefer total flexibility?
- Would you be OK if there was a rota to stick to?
- What do you need to fit in around work?
- What other commitments do you have that you want to be able to do?

_____

_____

_____

The role:

- What sort of role are you looking for — is it really the same as what you are doing now?
- Are there aspects of your current job or past roles that you really loved?
- What level do you want?
- Is this a promotion you are looking for?
- Are you looking for a sideways move?
- New sector?
- New responsibilities?

Culture:

- What is the type of organisation you ideally want to be working for?
- Is it fun? Serious? Worthy? Hardworking? Technically innovative? Environmentally friendly? Is it traditional in approach? Is the approach to Diversity + Inclusion, LBGTQ+, Black Lives Matter campaigns important — how do they talk about those issues?
- Should they be open to change and being flexible, or do you want more stability?
- Are they passionate about what they do or are they happy to just turn up and do their job?
- Do your passions align?

People:

- What size of organisation?
- What size of team?
- If managing people, what size? How many direct reports?
- What's your ideal manager like?
- What is the people side of life like? Social? Do you want a social life as well? After-work clubs? Sports? Activities? Fundraising? Community?
- What do you want by way of training / development?
- What do you want their approach to their people to be?

_____

_____

_____

_____

Package / Salary:

Finally, we come to package and salary. Often it is the first thing we look at along with a job title. Here, though, we are looking at the other attributes of the role FIRST.

Then you can add what salary you NEED to have — do the Hourly Rate Calculator Exercise later in the chapter to work out what this is.

You don't want to undersell yourself, but you also want to have the LIFE you want alongside this job, this career.

Package is not all about base salary. Many organisations offer other things within a package that can be really valuable depending on what you want.

If you want lots of holiday, then an organisation that offers 30 days a year will be more appealing than one which offers 23.

The base salary might be the same or it might be higher at the organisation offering 23 days. However, if holiday is a non-negotiable, you'll want the 30 days' holiday.

Then there are other things like pension contributions and affordable private health insurance.

- What is the market rate for this role?
- What salary do I NEED?
- What salary do I WANT?
- Number of days holiday I WANT / NEED
- Pension
- Healthcare
- Life insurance
- Discounts / Offers

_____

_____

_____

_____

_____

Go through each area and make a note of what is the ideal. What other benefits are of importance to you?

_____

You can come back to this exercise and add to it as other items occur to you. Take some time to review and reflect what you noted down. Is this a true reflection of everything you REALLY want? Have you missed anything out? Are you afraid of writing something down that you really want to do? This is a time for dreaming and writing it all down – no matter what it is.

 # Case Study

Sunetra

Sunetra was feeling very stuck and emotional about her search. She was coming out of a very toxic culture, one where everyone was blamed. Pressure was everywhere. Bullying was rife. People were leaving and stress levels throughout the whole organisation were off the chart.

The danger was that she was SO upset and SO angry and SO out of her comfort zone that the pendulum might swing too far. Often when we are in crisis mode we almost want to throw the towel in and say 'No more! I will just give up work and be a housewife'. I used to do that; when I was ill I used to say to my husband that I would become a teaching assistant for the school hours and the holidays. (I'd be no good at it, but I just saw it as an escape route.)

I wondered if this was what Sunetra was doing and wanted to make sure that she was not going to swing away from her true skills and values to something much safer simply because of how much she was suffering at the moment.

I helped her to do the Dream Job Mind Map Exercise. I asked her to remember the roles she had loved to get her thinking about a more positive environment, away from the current situation. Yes, it could tell us a lot about what she didn't want, but I wanted her to focus on what she did want. We would get better information from the more positive place of thinking.

She started to open up and think about her ideal day, her ideal manager, the culture and what she really wanted to achieve. As she spoke, the stress melted away because the toxicity of her current role started to recede. She started to remember what she was good at, when she had achieved great things, the last time she had fun in her role, with people she liked. Her face lit up and she became more animated as she spoke.

Location was important to her; she wanted to be more local, to have less of a commute that would add stress to her day. She wanted invigorating trips to London, on occasion. Not every day. She wanted the buzz that would give her.

We looked at the type of tasks she enjoyed doing, not just what experience might come up in a job description.

She wanted to make a difference; she wanted purpose. She liked engagement, she liked people, she wanted to host events where people could learn something and get engaged.

She wanted a safer space, with a more inclusive culture. A place where people could make mistakes but grow with it and not be blamed. She wanted action orientated organisations that achieved things.

After the session, Sunetra reflected that her energy was very different when talking about a different job, one she actually could imagine having a good time at.

My best job description...

If you were to write your own ideal job description, what would it say?

As you will have just explored in the Dream Job Mind Map Exercise, you will have come up with a lot of ideas as to what you want in a role. Now is the time to piece it together to find out what you would really be looking for in a role description when it comes up on a job search website or on LinkedIn.

Often job descriptions outline the type of work, the organisation, the culture and an element of what additional extras are expected.

 # Exercise

Best Job Description

Use the template to get some ideas and see what comes up.

- What do you notice?
- What is different about your current role to your dream?
- Are there any surprises?

Make a note of the things that you notice, and you can then refer back to these when you start to hone your job search.

My best job description

Job title
Job role
Location
Hours per week
Location
Travel required?

Role reports to — describe the leader you want to report to, the level they might be, what sort of leader do you want? How much time would you like with them, and what level of autonomy?

Role description — include responsibilities you really want (and note any you don't)

About the organisation — describe your ideal organisation, the culture, the people, the ethos

About the team — describe the team you'd love to work with, the sort of people, the energy you want, the collaboration, the style, how they communicate

Key objectives — what you want to be achieving in your role, what you are best at

Candidate skills — what skills have you got that you want to be using and showcasing in this role? (This is not your CV but include the key things you love and know you are good at that you want to be using more of.)

Additional skills to learn — what else do you want from this role? What additional experience?

Now that you have done the Dream Job Mind Map Exercise and the Best Job Description Exercise, it is time to reflect. Make a note of anything that comes up.

Take a look at your notes:

- What do you notice about your choices and ideas?

- Are there any surprises that have come up?

- Who can you speak to about the exercise? It can be helpful to talk through your thoughts with a partner, friend or coach to explore what has come up.

- Make a note of what your conclusions are.

 **Exercise**

Hourly Rate Calculator

Have you ever worked out your real hourly rate?

You may well know what hourly rate you are on if you work on that basis. For those of you on an annual salary we often don't calculate the exact hourly rate. But if you were to work out your hourly rate based on your contractual hours it would tell you your rate. What about if you worked it out based on your actual hours worked, and what about if you throw in the commute, the parking time, the lack of a lunch break? What do you think your rate would be then?

I mention this because whilst it might not be your prime reason for changing job, money can help us make decisions. When we tie it in with the Slice of Life Exercise it can be helpful to see what we are giving up for what additional amount of money.

Then – ask the question, is it worth it?

When looking for a new role, it might be at a lower salary, but if it is closer to home and allows you to go to the gym, then your hourly rate may well go up and your quality of life may well rise as well.

Here's an example:

Someone earning 36,000 a year, on a 37.5 hour a week contract for 5 days a week is earning an hourly rate of 18.46.

However, if that person never takes a lunch break and has a 2-hour daily commute (1 hour each way) then the hourly rate drops to 13.19.

If that person decided to take a better job, a job they really wanted nearer to home, where they could work from home a couple of days and take a lunch break daily, they could afford to drop the base salary to 27,000 in order to keep the same hourly rate of 13.85.

But this time they would have gained 3 hours of time back for themselves. In addition, they would save 50 a week on commuting – 2,400 from their taxed income. The hourly rate is now 15.08.

Ideally, we want the same salary but less hours. Sounds impossible, right? But what if you were savvy about what you looked for and knew which things were non-negotiable? Could you work from home at a different organisation and save the time and the commuting costs?

What is your hourly rate?

Take some time to work out your hourly rate for the contracted number of hours worked.

Then work out all the additional hours you do — consider commute, lunch breaks that you work, weekend work, email checking etc. Remember to deduct any other outgoings from your base salary that are deducted from source such as pension contributions, student loan repayments, healthcare or other benefits.

Contracted hourly rate: _____

Actual hourly rate: _____

_____

 **Exercise**

Budget Calculator

Working backwards can be helpful here

Sometimes when we look for work, we assume that we always have to be asking for more money, more responsibility, a bigger team. However, when was the last time you worked out what you really needed to earn? Most of us live beyond our means and most of us spend what we earn. If we earn less, we'd spend less. Earn more, we find ways of spending it.

But let's not go grab a job just to pay bills we don't even want to have. To buy stuff we don't need. What do we really want?

Time to go back to basics:

Use the sheet below to write down every cost / bill / outgoing.

Item	Amount per month	Want / Need going forward Y/N
Mortgage		
Electricity		
Water		
Council tax		
Gas		
Broadband		
Mobile phone		
Cleaners		
Gardeners		
Childcare / Nursery		
Elderly care		
Car insurance		
Car loan		
Petrol		
Other loans / debt		
Student loan		
Car repairs		
Holidays		
Train tickets — season ticket		
Train tickets — other		
House repairs		
Computer / Technology		
Stationery / Office supplies		
Glasses		
Other health costs / prescriptions		
BUPA / Health insurance		
Netflix / Amazon Prime subscriptions		
Food — basics		
Food — takeaways		
Food — luxury items		
Alcohol — in-house		
Pub / Going out		
Books		
Make-up / Toiletries		
Newspapers		
Gym membership		
Online subscriptions		
Other classes / study		
Clothes		
Bedding		
Cleaning materials		

Are there things on this list that you are spending money on because of your job?

There are obvious ones like petrol or a train ticket but what about other hidden costs? Are you spending a fortune on internet shopping due to stress? Is the gym membership there to keep you sane, but ideally, you'd like time for a walk? Are you spending money on spa days, treatments and the like just to allow you to return to work?

What if you turned those off? How much would you need to earn then?

> *I realised that I was paying for a chiropractor every week to sort my back out, which was caused by stress. I was also going to a local spa every month to 'escape' and I had a yoga membership to allow me to meditate so that I could cope. The cost of that was a massive £4,280 per year from my taxed income! If I turned those off, I could take a pay cut of over £5,000 and be happier and have all that time back. What might you be spending just to prop yourself up in your current job?*

What do you really want to be doing and really spending your money on?

_____

 **Summary**

In this section you have done a lot of thinking and a lot of dreaming big!

Make sure you capture all your thoughts from the sections:

1. Complete the 'Slice of Life' Exercise
2. Complete the 'Feeling the Future' Exercise
3. Work through the 'Dream Job Mind Map' Exercise
4. Complete the 'Best Job Description' Exercise
5. Work out your own hourly rate using the 'Hourly Rate Calculator' Exercise
6. Look at the 'Budget Calculator' Exercise

Chapter 7

What am I good at?

YOU HAVE DONE a huge amount of thinking already about yourself, your values and your dream role. Well done! I hope you have had a few tea breaks and some gaps in between to rest your brain and reflect on everything you have done so far.

In this chapter we are going to be working on:

- Discovering what you are naturally talented at
- Finding out what your passions are
- Exploring everything you have experience in and are skilled at

Remember to take some breaks and come back to any section if you can't immediately think of what to write.

Skill sets and natural talents

*When my role was made redundant after 12 years in a senior position my first response was 'What the actual F***?!' I was shocked and upset and immediately went into denial.*

'This can't be happening to me...' 'This is my role.'

'I'm good at what I do.'

> *'Why??'*
>
> *Very quickly afterwards, though, I realised that I had an opportunity – to plan my new future, create a new life for myself. But my confidence had taken a knock and voices of self-doubt started to creep in.*

Whether your confidence has dropped due to redundancy, frustration, being overlooked or being badly managed, it can be hard to remember what you are good at and what you've done.

To be the best version of yourself when presenting your skills in your CV and talking about yourself at interview you need to know what you are good at. You need to remember what makes you good at what you do. This section is all about looking back, taking stock, and realising what skills, experience and talents you already have and can take forward into your next role.

Many people really underestimate what they are good at.

And not only that, they don't even know what it is about themselves that makes them good at what they do!

They'll say things like, *'Oh I just do that...'*

Maybe you've said something like this yourself?

'Oh, I just do that naturally.'

Or *'I never thought of it like that, this is just what I do.'*

And the classic:

'Doesn't everyone do it that way?'

And the answer is NO. Not everyone does it that way.

The first step is actually appreciating what you are good at. Maybe you are also someone who is doing brilliantly in certain areas, and yet you're not even mentioning it on your CV. It's because you take it for granted, that that's *just* what you do. It's just who you are.

'I'm always really brilliantly organised.'

'I'm always really passionate about my work.'

'I love communicating with people.'

You just haven't valued it before now. Maybe you've even forgotten some key experience from years ago that might be useful to mention NOW!

Finding your natural talents

When we go to a traditional performance review, we often get some question asking about our weaknesses or what needs improving. There is often a disproportionate attempt to move us from **unskilled** to **skilled**, rather than focus on what we are great at and to give us more of that type of work.

The diagram below shows that when we have **no skill / limited skill** the work is more difficult. Results are likely to be poorer and results are likely to be slower. Conversely, where we are **skilled** / a **natural** we will often get faster results with better quality and can be more creative.

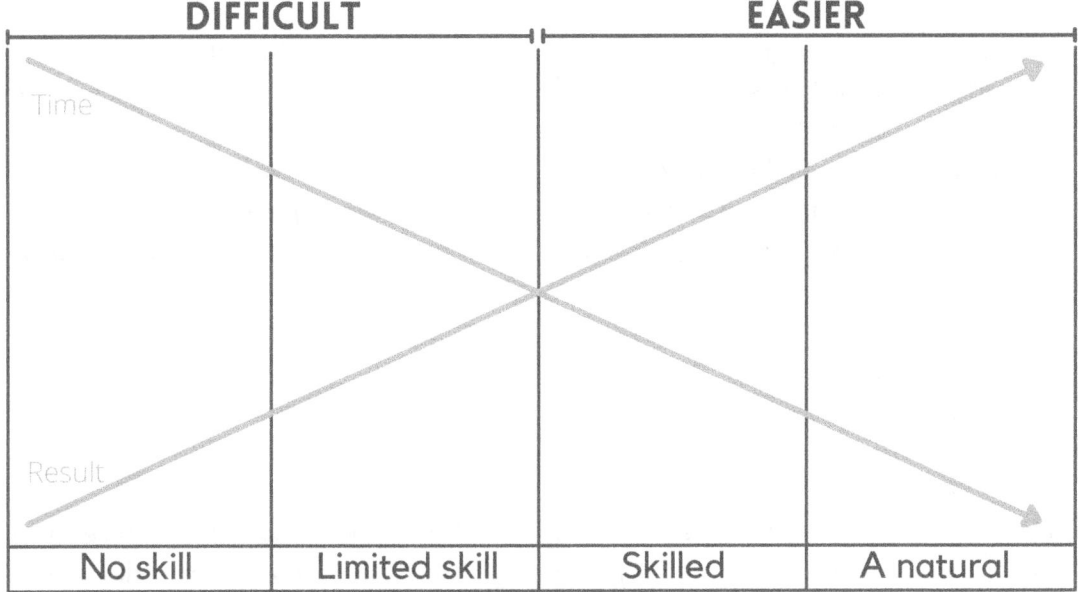

A traditional model of school and work is to go from **no skill** to **limited skill**, and then perhaps to get **skilled**. However, you could take me through 10 different courses on finance and accounting and I am really only ever going to reach **limited skill** level. I'm never going to be **a natural**.

We all start with **no skill** for most jobs that we initially start with. We all start with **limited skill** in management. Hopefully with some training, support and mentoring we can become **skilled**, and we might even find we've got **a natural** talent for it. Until we started learning, we didn't know that that was something available to us. There is a level of exploration and recognition of what feels right and what people give us praise and credit for as we develop.

Being **skilled** at something still isn't as good as using your **natural talents**. If you are using your natural, innate abilities, then the energy you put into doing something using your **natural talents** will shine through. You will perform better and outshine others.

So how do you know what your natural talents are?

Natural talents table

A natural	Skilled
- You create energy doing it; you are excited doing these things - You get a buzz from doing it - It is easy for you — you do it with no effort - You get amazing results without thinking - You often think this is *just* what people do - You always improve or are ahead of the curve - People are positive	- Performance is high standard - Others delegate to you as you are better at it than they are - Not difficult for you but you don't LOVE it - Reputation is great - Gives you opportunity to do more or work with others
Limited skill	**No skill**
- Newly acquired skill with limited experience - You get the job done - You need to put in a bit of energy but only get 'OK' results - Competition — others can do better than you - Can cause anxiety — you worry about getting it wrong - Repetition of task and you get bored	- Brand new to a task and no experience - No matter how hard you work you will never be good at it - You cannot do even if taught for hours - High effort for poor result - Can be perceived as a weakness - Can cause frustrations / stress / conflict and confusion

Read the table above and think about some of the tasks you do and which area they fit into. You can now start to fill in the blank table, below, with your own skills and talents.

 **Exercise**

Natural Talents

Natural talent	Skilled
Limited skill	No skill

Taking action:

Take 5 minutes to start to think about your own skill sets. Jot down any areas where you can easily establish which box that task, or work element, fits into.

Chapter 7: What am I good at?

Then take a more detailed look at your skills and talents. There are some questions and prompts to help you think below. Don't worry if you can't remember everything at once; come back to it.

Think about when you last got a feeling of pure buzz, that energy, that excitement that might show you an area of natural talent.

- What sort of thing were you doing?

  _____

  _____

- What element of that task or work was it that got your attention? What specific element?

  _____

  _____

  _____

- Don't just think of big things like 'projects' or 'communicating' or 'people' — delve deeper. What was it about those projects, the communications, the people?

  _____

  _____

  _____

Questions to consider:

In projects:

Was it writing the presentations, was it talking to people, was it problem solving, was it being creative, was it the challenge, the people, the atmosphere?

Was it the start of the project that you liked? Was it the data collection? Was it the analysis? Was it the project meetings? Was it the close down of the project, the lessons learned, or the implementation, the launch, or the marketing?

Look at projects that you got involved in and just think about the things that you loved.

In communications:

You could think about communications that you like or don't like. Do you like Zoom or other online meetings, or hate them?

Or do you get a buzz from standing up and presenting in front of lots of people?

What about stakeholders and customers; do you enjoy meeting with customers? Do you have a natural talent at sorting out customer complaints, customer problems, sticky issues? Are you a great salesperson?

Do you prefer one-to-one chats, formal or informal?

Do you write excellent communications?

Do you always spot typos or formatting errors?

Do you write presentations with flair?

In people:

Do you like managing people? Are you good at it?

What aspects of people management do you like? Is it the motivational side? The delegation? Are you the carer, the teacher, the nurturer? Do you notice body language and energy?

Do you like team results, team spirit? Do you like crisis management?

Maybe it is recruiting a new team or starting something from scratch?

Do you love selling change and creating something new?

Perhaps you like mentoring, coaching and training?

Other considerations:

Where do you get asked to help at work?

What were you actually doing in those scenarios?

What else just comes naturally to you? Where people are always saying to you, 'Oh, you're so good at that'?

Do you train people on tasks, because you're just the brilliant person in the office who can always show people exactly how to do something technically? Are you the whizz kid who can fix anything?

> *A recent coaching client found a job that was the perfect match for her. Within six months, she had already been promoted. That was because she'd really worked on what her passions were. She turned up so enthusiastic about the job that the new leaders could see that she was a really great fit to the organisation and culture. They could then see the potential in her for doing the next level job. All because she'd matched her natural talents to the role.*

What areas would you like to be doing but need more skill at? Sometimes we might need to complete a course or do some refresher training to get to where we want to be. Make a note of any areas of development that are essential for your future dream role.

Other resources to explore

Have a look at your old CVs and your past LinkedIn profile for inspiration. Review old jobs that you loved (and those that you were happy to move on from). What do they tell you about your skills and talents?

- There might be patterns you've not seen before.
- What elements of previous roles did you really like?
- What gave you a buzz there?
- You might find some themes that you've always liked.

Take a look at your past performance review paperwork. It might highlight some of your weaknesses, and you might want to put those items into the **no skill, limited skill areas**. It'll also tell you some things that you've done well, and they might give you an indication of whether they are things you are **skilled** at or whether they are **natural talents**.

Have a look at what feedback you are getting. Make a note and collate it all.

What about any praise, rewards, employee of the month awards? Never be dismissive of praise! Capture it and keep it! Don't brush it off — make a note!

Think about what people are actually saying to you and think about what it was that you did that made them so happy.

Because it's *'just what you do'*.

The opposite side of the coin

Now to make a note of things you don't like. It is worth looking at both ends of the spectrum here.

What you dislike about work, people, tasks and situations can also tell you a lot about what you don't want your new job to be too!

This is the stuff that you find sticky, tricky. Where you have to restart things, perhaps there are mistakes in it, or you get pulled up for something because it's not quite right. Put those on the other side in the **No skill** or **Limited skill** box. It's OK to put things in there — we can't be good at everything!

 **Exercise**

Finding Your Passion

This exercise is about starting to think about what it is that you're passionate about and how you can then identify it, put it forward into your job search and CV and talk confidently about it in your interview.

Here's a model that I use in my coaching practice, to help you work out where you are and how you feel when doing what you do.

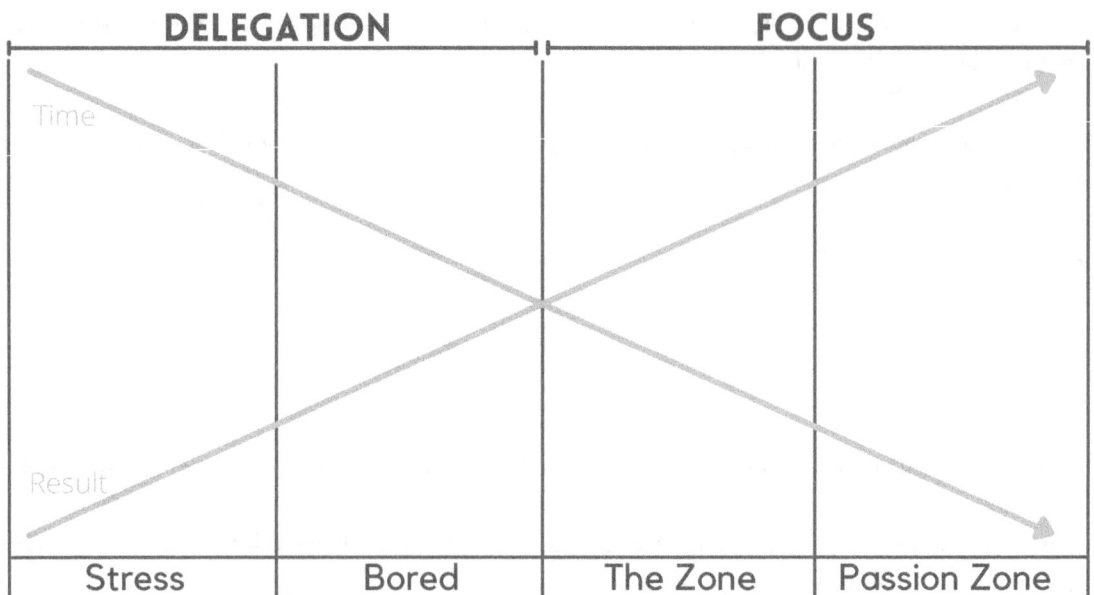

I've broken work life into these different zones.

The Stress Zone

We can probably all recognise the Stress Zone. This is where the work makes you anxious, worried, stressed. You're more likely to be making mistakes, where you don't know where to start. A bit of confusion, perhaps even panic.

What you find is that in the Stress Zone, it takes longer to do things and the results are poorer. The 'result' line is at its lowest and the 'time' taken is at its highest. It is definitely something to consider not doing or delegating if it is part of your role.

The Bored Zone

You know how to do the work, but you find it boring and bland and of no interest or importance to you.

As you move along the scale to the right, there might be some things that you could be quite good at. But they don't excite you. They still probably take a bit more time because you lack interest and because you are still a bit bored you might make mistakes; you might miss something out. The results will still be low. You're probably not going to be thinking very creatively or with any energy. It's worth looking at delegation options here too.

THE Zone

You can FEEL when you are in **'The Zone'**; you're just itching to get stuff done.

You crack on with things easily. These might be things you naturally turn to first thing every day. These are the things you like; you can get them done quicker, you can get better results, you're perhaps doing it better than the next person who's doing the same sort of job as you.

And it's likely to be something that you like. You can find yourself buzzing around and getting on, and you're probably getting better results than other people.

What you find is that in THE Zone, it takes a bit less time and with better results and you just whip through things.

The Passion Zone

Finally, you have got the real sweet spot, which is the **Passion Zone**.

You just love this stuff!!! It's the work that you just do naturally. It's the tasks that people ask you to do, or you volunteer to do. You might just find that this is when you feel completely in the flow.

This is what you love; you just adore it!

And in this zone, you're going to be getting much better results than the average person, and you're going to be doing it really quickly, flying through the tasks. You'll see that here the 'time' line is at its lowest and the 'results' line is at its highest. Big results for less time.

Which zone are you in?

Using the template, start to think about what proportion of time you are spending in each of these areas in your current role.

Write down a rough percentage of your day, week or month that you are spending in each of those areas. What proportion are you in the Stress or Bored Zone, and how much of your day is really making you excited, passionate and fulfilled?

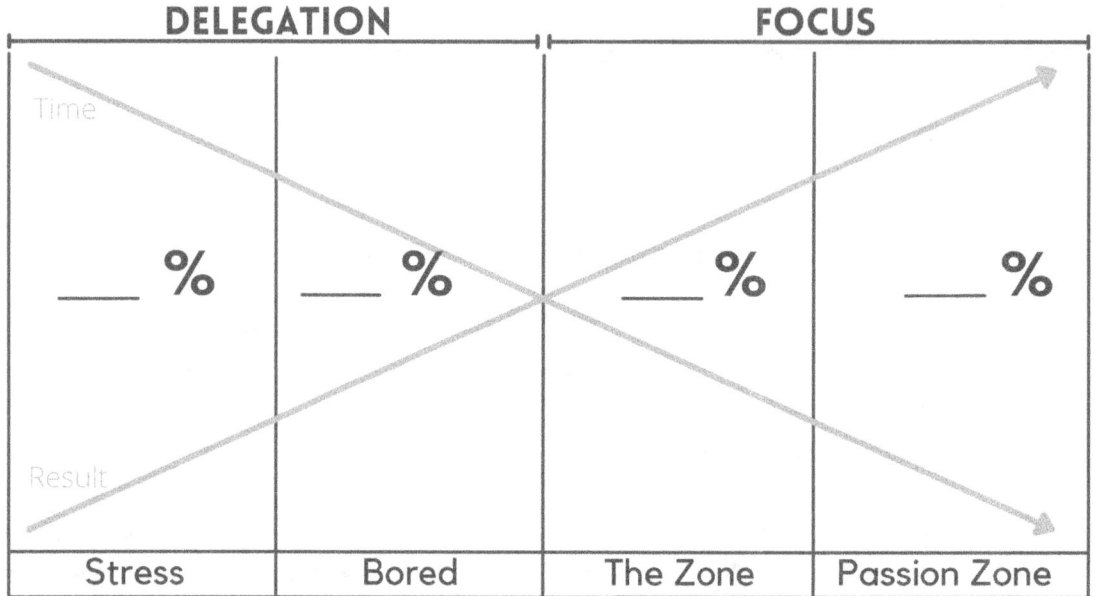

Now imagine your ideal set-up. What would you like it to be? What proportion would be a better fit for you?

In many roles, there may well be things that you can't completely avoid. For example, in my Operations Director roles, I knew I had to have *some* finance responsibility, but I would always aim to delegate what I could. I would want to make sure it was a very small proportion of my overall job description.

Which zones do you want to be in?

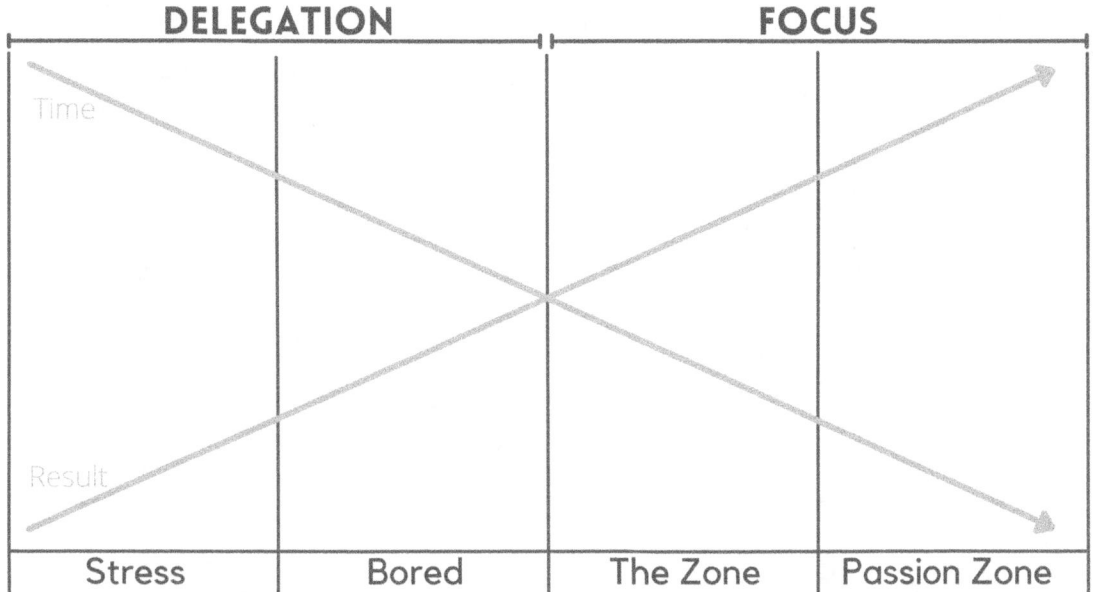

Next, fill in the types of tasks that you recognise are in each of the zones. Look at your current job, but also take some time to look at past jobs to identify areas you really enjoyed or those you really disliked.

DELEGATION		FOCUS	
Stress	Bored	The Zone	Passion Zone

For me I realised something needed to change when I found that a lot of my tasks were causing me to be in the Stress Zone. I was dealing with politics, finances. Ultimately, I know I can do it. I've had to run big budgets in my time. But I don't particularly like looking at finance reports. I certainly don't like presenting finance reports. If I had to look at them a lot, I'd probably be in the Bored Zone. If I had to do a big presentation on that topic that would probably put me in the Stress Zone.

The interesting thing is it would also take me much longer to create something in the finance space. If I had to pull together some spreadsheets or a big budget, it would take me ages and the result might be poorer than if I delegated it and gave it to somebody who loves it. It's why my accountant husband does my books!

If you could do more of your job in **the Zone** or in the **Passion Zone**, and find a job that matched those areas, then you would have more enthusiasm and you'd be more productive. In addition, you would be better able to demonstrate to your employer that you're really good at your job, that you get great results.

Delegation option

Now, if you're in a job at the moment where you've got some things in the Stress or Bored Zone, one potential solution, if it's open to you, is to look at whether you can delegate. You might not need to jump ship and get another job.

It can be helpful to draw a huge circle on a piece of paper for this exercise.

Take a look at everything you are doing. Write down everything you SHOULD be doing inside the circle. And write down everything that you SHOULD NOT be doing outside the circle.

- What do you notice about what is in and out of the circle?
- What can you stop doing?
- What can you ask others to do?
- What things are you doing that others are supposed to be doing anyway?
- How much chasing, checking, and reworking are you doing?

Exploring your experiences

 **Case Study**

Simon

Simon came to me when his role was made redundant after many years as a head teacher.

He was angry. He was bitter. He was lost. He wasn't sure what he was going to do next.

He wanted to work on a plan for the future. He was worried that the head teacher 'label' meant that he was not going to be able to transfer into the business world.

Interestingly Simon forgot all of his past experience before becoming a head teacher. When we started to look at what skills he had, he was focussed only on the head teacher role. It was the closest experience he could remember. I asked him to go further back in time.

There can be trends and themes when we look at our overall career that can tell us something. Even if we know that we don't want to do that particular role again.

I asked Simon what he had been doing before getting the head role. He had been a commercial director! He'd just forgotten. I set him some homework to look at all of the training certificates he'd done. He had done various counselling certificates, health and safety, wellbeing, coaching. I asked him to look back into the past and list every business he'd been involved in from the year dot. What had he done, what roles had he taken on? What experience had that given him? What did he want to do now — really?

He did the Slice of Life Exercise. At one point he asked me with a wry smile, 'What is a hobby?' He had spent every waking hour in school as part of the head teacher responsibility. He didn't have time for exercise, his family, or any other activities that he loved. I asked him to take some time to flesh out what his new life was going to look like.

He came back the next week and explained that he wanted to work much fewer hours, and he wanted to have a 'hobby / family' day. He wanted to make a difference to people. He wanted to use his experience in child welfare for good. He wanted to be in a business rather than in the education sector. He realised that he had a lot more senior business experience than he had thought and so he felt more confident going for a business sector role.

Once he knew what he wanted he was able to start talking to his friends and picked up old relationships and explained the sort of thing he was looking for. He spoke with huge passion and energy and one conversation led him to an introduction with an organisation who were looking for someone just like him.

 **Exercise**

Experience Finder

When we have been head down in a role for a number of years it can be easy to forget some of the key experiences from our past roles that have shaped us into who we are today.

The purpose of this exercise is to track back through our career and experience and remember everything that might be useful to us now.

Depending on how many roles you have had this may take a while! I'd urge you not to rush this stage. If you have started to uncover what your dream job might be in the previous chapter, it will be helpful to give you a good steer as to the sort of experience you might want to resurrect. Like Simon in the case study above, he knew he wanted to get back into a senior management role and rediscovered his previous experience as a sales director when he looked back. What relevant skills might you be able to dust down and polish up?

You can choose to either start at your current job and work backwards, or you can start at the beginning of your career and work forwards, whichever method works for you. For this section you might find a separate notebook or blank sheets of paper useful as you scroll back over the years.

It can be helpful here to look at your CV, LinkedIn and any other information you have to hand, such as training certificates, course information or qualifications. Everything is useful at this stage.

There are spaces here for you to note down your conclusions.

Key skills from the past

_____

_____

_____

_____

Key skills I want to re-use

_____
_____
_____

Key skills I want to brush up on

_____
_____
_____

Key qualifications and training that might be useful

_____
_____
_____

Key skills I have that will be great for my dream job

_____
_____
_____

Now we will explore your skills and experience from a couple of other angles, to see if there are any other areas that might come to light.

Challenging moments

This might sound strange, but one of my favourite things used to be when days went wrong. I would get a real buzz out of being a trouble-shooter. Back before remote working was a thing, I managed a call centre of 100 people. Whenever there was a snow day and everyone was sitting in the office looking out the window thinking, 'Oh, well, we're going to get sent home', you couldn't just say to everyone, right, pack and leave; we had to do it all in a staggered, planned way.

Me and a couple of my colleagues used to love those days because there was something new to do. It was a challenge. It was exciting. There was a bit of drama. Other people would have potentially hated that kind of panic and something going wrong.

Equally, when sometimes the call centre telephony system broke down or there was a big outage, I quite liked marching around and trying to find out what went on and getting stuff done and being the trouble-shooter to resolve it.

That would be in my Passion Zone and my natural talent area.

You might think God, that sounds absolutely horrendous.

What are those things that you say? 'Yes, yes, this is great? I absolutely love doing those things'?

 **Exercise**

Challenging Moments

What challenges do you secretly love when they come up?

Make a note of anything out of the ordinary that you can think of.

___

___

___

___

___

Outside of work

You can also start to look outside of work. I don't know if you've watched MasterChef? It always amazes me that nearly every year on MasterChef, there is someone who is in their 40s or 50s.

Gregg and John say, 'So why are you appearing on the programme?' And the contestant says, 'Well, I've always wanted to be a chef, always absolutely loved cooking. But my parents told me I had to become a lawyer or a doctor but now I've got burnt out at that, I've decided I've had enough and I'm going to become a chef.' And they're usually brilliant at it because they're naturally talented and passionate about it. But they just had to put that in a box for 20/30 years. And now they're coming back to it.

What are you doing outside of work that you love and really want to turn into a role?

You might decide that these are things you never really want to do in work. But it can just give you a little bit of an insight. It might not be your next career. It might also tell you something about how you like to work and what sort of things you would prefer to be doing.

For example, a coaching client who wanted to be more creative concluded that whilst they would like a more creative job, they were creative in their life outside of work. They decided that it was okay because they were covering the creative bases on one side of their life; they didn't need to change their role to meet that need. However, it did show them that they had a creative mindset that they could use in their workplace more than they had been doing to date.

By getting *more* creativity in work, then they might move into the **Passion Zone** more than before.

Think of the other areas such as hobbies like cooking, writing, gaming, technology, photography or whatever else you do outside of work. Note them down.

_____

_____

_____

_____

_____

External responsibilities

What activities do you do outside of work which have additional responsibility? Are you forgetting about those things and not even putting them on your CV? As well as being interesting things to note down for your CV or interview stories, they can also tell you more about where your passions and **natural talents** lie. What have you naturally gravitated to in those roles? What can they tell you about your **natural talents** and your energy levels?

Perhaps you are a school governor, a trustee or volunteer for a charity, or you might do local fundraising.

Why do you do those roles?

___

Things to consider:

Is it the fact that you're making a difference to people?

___

Is it the fact that you're so good at fundraising because you're a natural salesperson, and you're great at communicating?

___

What gives you the energy when doing those roles?

___

What other roles or responsibilities do you have outside of work that are being overlooked?

___

Are you doing other things such as caring for children, elderly relatives, parents, or organising family life? What areas of those responsibilities come naturally to you, that you naturally pick up because you are 'the best person for the job'?

___

Review all areas; some things you might *have* to do but dislike, but for other things, you might think, there's a real bit of a passion there.

___

Ask others

Sometimes we really don't know ourselves. It can be hard to hold a mirror up and think, 'What is it I'm good at?' We are often very dismissive of what we are good at. If someone pays us a compliment, we brush it off, and we can be very self-deprecating.

> One of my coaching clients told me, 'When questioning what to do with my career I found it really helpful to find people that I could talk to. Not just my usual mates, but those who would be challenging and help with the direction I might want to go, without shooting myself in the foot!' He explored who he could talk to, saying, 'I found a couple of people who were interested in helping me and they were not only supportive, reminding me what I was good at, but asked me difficult questions whilst challenging me at the same time. Having that outlet helped me to reflect on what I really wanted.'

Think about who you might be able to ask for feedback. Which of your friends is always reminding you of what you are good at? Which of your nearest and dearest can be relied upon to give you a boost?

Note down what they tell you:

_____

_____

_____

_____

Ask colleagues

Think about whether you might be able talk to colleagues, either past or present.

If you've kept in touch with old colleagues perhaps they would be able to remind you of some past achievements.

You could use LinkedIn and consider asking people for a recommendation, or direct message them and ask for feedback if you feel comfortable.

Ask family

If you are feeling brave, you could ask your family.

Now, they might know what you don't like, because you might be moaning about the bad day you've had or your annoying manager!

They might not tell you all the successes that you have had, but they might know that you don't like certain aspects of your job. So that might be useful to note down.

Ask managers

If you feel comfortable, you can ask your line manager about where they think you are more **naturally talented**, or the most **skilled**. You might have covered that in annual reviews or at performance review time. Even if you don't want to ask them directly, you can now tune in to what they are saying about what went well.

Chapter 7: What am I good at?

Ask coach / mentor

If you have them around you, consider external people like coaches and mentors who might be able to reflect on past conversations with you.

Past challenges and what you've dealt with

When I did my diploma with the AoEC (The Academy of Executive Coaching), they asked me to answer the question, 'Who am I and how do I coach?'

At first, I gave some very high-level answers — I am a good listener, I am an experienced leader.

The tutors pushed me harder! Why was I really like that? What experiences in life had made me the person I really am? After a lot of thinking and pushing myself (and a few tears), I discovered that all of my life experiences I'd gone through as a child, a teenager, a mother and a career woman had shaped how I coach.

Having a mother who tried to commit suicide meant that I understood the importance of looking out for mental health issues; it's where I developed empathy.

Earlier experiences at home meant that I could tune in to body language and mood; it's where I developed insight.

As I got older, my role was made redundant. I learnt how devastating it was to feel cast aside. I learnt that it could feel like grief, and takes time to overcome. I learnt patience and about taking positive action.

When I had children, I experienced discrimination. I learnt about unfairness and battling on. I got promoted and saw the benefit of having a coach and a sponsor. I learnt what good leadership looks like.

When my youngest child got ill, I decided that a long commute was no longer viable and I changed jobs, dropping 20k in salary and two job grades to be nearer home. I learnt about priorities.

When my chronic migraines knocked me over and I had to go on long-term sick, I changed my working hours and put my health first. I learnt about work-life balance. I learnt about my own health.

 **Exercise**

Past Challenges

What things have you had to deal with in your past that have made you stronger, more skilled, or aware than you were before? What life events have meant that you've had to take stock, or learn something or become more resilient? What skills have those events taught you?

Things to consider:

- What have you dealt with in your life that has made you who you are?
- What have you done that you never thought you'd manage?
- Where are you most resilient?
- Sometimes the biggest challenges in life can be the things that shape us more than we realise.
- What experiences would you be bringing to a new role?

_____

_____

_____

_____

_____

_____

_____

 **Summary**

By now you'll be starting to build a picture of your own skill sets, talents, likes and dislikes.

Make sure you have:

1. Discovered your natural talents
2. Discovered your passions
3. Identified your experiences
4. Looked at past challenges that have shaped you
5. Reviewed your external responsibilities for any clues

Now we can get ready to pull everything together into your **ideal job checklist**.

Chapter 8

Creating your ideal job checklist

Creating your checklist

AS YOU'VE GONE through the exercises so far, you'll have been gathering information about your preferences and criteria for the job you really want. Having your **ideal job checklist** can save you time, effort and energy and stop you from applying for jobs that are not a good fit.

Using the **ideal job checklist** can ensure that you get the right job alerts coming through, can help you screen which job interview invitations you want and finally allow you to review job offers to ensure that you get the best fit possible.

Doing this before starting the search and certainly before spending time applying can be crucial.

We can get carried away with the shiny package on offer and before we know it, we've accepted a job with occasional travel to America because it offered 20k more, without thinking about the consequences.

Go back through each of the exercises and make sure you have reviewed your notes from the exercises in Chapter 7. Note which are the really key elements you identified. You can now start to add these conclusions to the **ideal job checklist**.

Once you've noted down your ideal job requirements, think about what you would and would not accept for that category.

For example, location:

Ideally you might want to work two days in the office and three days at home.

You would accept three days in the office and two at home.

But you would NOT accept four or five days in the office.

Highlight any particular categories that are 'non-negotiables' — without them you wouldn't even consider the job. You can highlight with a star or a colour, but make sure you have recognised which are the most important items for you.

In the example below, I have highlighted travel as a non-negotiable with a star. I could work a few more hours in a bigger company but I know I definitely do NOT want to travel.

Here is an example template to show you how it can help to structure your thoughts.

My ideal job checklist			
Item	Ideal set-up	Acceptable set-up	Not acceptable
Location	2 days in office / 3 days at home	3 in office / 2 at home	4 / 5 in office
*Travel (non-negotiable)	None	Occasional trips to London	Weekly + trips to London or national or international travel
Number of hours	25	Up to 30	Over 30
Size of organisation	25–50 people	<250	>1000
Commute	Walking distance (2 miles)	Local – bus / car with parking) (10 miles)	Train / London (plus 30 miles or over 30 mins)

You can use the blank template overleaf to add the elements that are relevant for you to your own table from the list below. Feel free to add anything else that is important to you. You can also download blank templates from www.dellajudd.co.uk/bookresources.

Other criteria to consider:

Location: WFH — number of days / Office-based / Hybrid
Number of hours: 37.5 / 30 / 25
Hours of work: start at 8 finish at 4 / 9–5 / 10–6 / 8–1
Working week: Part time / Full time / Condensed / Shifts
Working week: Mon–Fri / Mon off / No weekends / Evenings only
Number of days' holiday: 23 / 25 / 30 — option to buy additional days
Benefits: Pension / Insurance / Healthcare / Car / Other key items you want
Sector: Private / Corporate / Charity / SME
Size of org: Small / Medium / Large (number of employees)
Size of org: Global / European / UK / Regional / Local
Travel: None / Some / A lot
Travel: National / International / Europe / Local
Travel frequency: Daily / Weekly / Monthly
Commute: None (WFH) / Less than 30 mins / 3–60 mins / 60–90 mins / 90mins +
Commute: Drive / Train / Bus / Walk
Culture of org: Ambitious / Stable / Technically modern / Caring / Learning culture / Corporate responsibility / Environment / Profitability / Leadership style / Purpose / Fun / Sociable
Culture of org: Values desired
Ideal Manager: Visible / Autonomy given / Supportive / Mentor / Driven / Coaching style
Training: Available / Sponsorships / Approach to training
Role: Challenging / New / Stable / Changing / Processing / Strategic / Comfortable
Using skills: List skills crucial to be used
Salary: Preferred level / Min
Team: Scale and size — (being part of a team) Small / Medium / Large
Leadership of a team — Small / Medium / Large / None
Budget responsibility — Yes / No
Budget responsibility — Small / Medium / Large
Responsibilities — what do you want to have responsibility for
Responsibilities — what do you NOT want to have responsibility for

My ideal job checklist			
Item	Ideal set-up	Acceptable set-up	Not acceptable

My ideal job checklist			
Item	Ideal set-up	Acceptable set-up	Not acceptable

By the end of the process, you will have a complete **ideal job checklist** of key things you are looking for as well as your highlighted non-negotiables.

Take a look at your list.

Does it feel right? Does it look exciting to you?

Don't worry yet about whether that role exists; just focus on the feeling that this type of role and set-up gives you. If there are any uncertain areas, take some time out and ponder those areas. If need be, go back to the exercises and relook at what came up during those. Have you compromised along the way? Is there some other aspect that you hadn't considered?

Hone the checklist until you feel it has captured everything and feels right. Take some time to do this. The answers may come very easily to you, after the thinking you have done before, or it may take some time to percolate and filter through. Don't worry and don't rush the answers. If you are someone who likes to chat through your thoughts, find a friend who you can express yourself to, and chat over your ponderings. If you like to write, then use this book or another journal to write down what is coming up for you. You might be a deep thinker; if so, allow yourself the space and time to allow the thinking to happen, in the knowledge that the answers will come.

You can always change the list and you can cross things off and add to it as circumstances change or you make new decisions.

 Case Study

Ashley

Ashley was frustrated with internal politics, restructures and a manager who was both controlling and often absent. Initially our coaching was focussed on wellbeing – he was stressed, not sleeping and working all hours to keep up. Once we worked on getting his health back on an even keel, Ashley realised that some of the situations that were causing the wellbeing issues were not going to go away and he started to explore the idea of moving organisation.

Ashley had started looking at LinkedIn and job sites and was tempted to apply immediately for things, even though as a recruiter he would often advise candidates not *'to jump ship just to jump ship'*. Applying in desperation never usually ends well.

We started by doing the Dream Job Mind Map Exercise and Ashley was able to really start thinking about what he WANTED, something he had not done up to now. Things like location and sector came up as important considerations as well as the culture and the vibe of any target companies.

'I started to think about what it was that I wanted to get out of the job, not just the job title or the job itself,' he said. *'I realised where I didn't want to go. The job hunt was easier because you can disappear into a LinkedIn black hole – all the jobs look great, but they are not a great match with what you want.'*

The process *'changed my thinking and I started to build my own internal check list of what I wanted as well as what I didn't want'*. Fairly soon after the exercises were complete, Ashley was approached by someone referring him to a role, and he could immediately weigh it up against the checklist and see that it was a great match.

He then paused so that he could do the research into the organisation by looking at LinkedIn, Glassdoor and talking to a few people he knew who either worked there or had worked there before. Because he knew what he was looking for he was able to articulate that to his friends and say – *'Do you think I will get these things from a role there?'*

Once those additional checks on the culture, the vibe, the strategy, were passed he could then turn to the application with enthusiasm.

Ashley's advice: *'Do the checklist before you start your job search; you don't want to waste your time on pointless applications.'*

Ashley identified the really important non-negotiable items as well as a list of grey areas, where he could go either way, depending on the offer. He also had his list of 'nice to haves' and absolute no's!

He concluded, '*Applying for jobs is hard, especially after a tough day. By limiting the search, you can save time, energy and emotional stress. Rejections can hit you hard — so only applying for realistic roles and jobs that you know you match and really want can reduce the levels of disappointment.*'

 **Exercise**

Key Date Planner

Now you know what your ideal job checklist looks like, let's revisit your plan.

What dates are relevant to your search now?

___

___

___

___

___

___

___

Things to consider:

When do you want a new job by — realistically?

What dates are you now working to?

_____

Ideal new start date: _____

What is your notice period (if any): _____

When will you start your search? _____

What dates are you available for interviews? _____

When is your first available start date (good to have this in your mind before you start the interview process)?

_____

_____

 # Summary

The checklist is going to be your handy tool that you will use throughout your application, interview and offer process. Consider making it in a format that is easy for you to refer back to. Use Excel, Word or create your own on paper, that you can keep looking at.

Make sure you have:

1. Looked at all of the **ideal job checklist** criteria and noted your own requirements

2. Considered your non-negotiables

3. Considered the grey area items and what you will and won't accept for certain categories

Chapter 9
Telling others

SO, YOU'VE DONE the work, done the reflections and created an **ideal job checklist** that you are excited about. You have your idea of a dream job, where it will be and what you will be doing. You know where your passions lie and what you want to get up for in the morning.

But. There is just one thing. You need to bring the people around you on board.

At first glance it can feel easy to say that this is your dream, and you will follow it. But it isn't as easy as that. There are things to consider, people to consider, other lives to think about and how your decisions might impact them.

You want this to work, and you want to enjoy your job AND your home life too. No point in getting your dream job only for other aspects to start to crumble.

Taking some time now to explain what you want to your nearest and dearest can really help. You'll need support along the way and if everyone around you can understand what you are doing and why, then you will feel more energised and able to do your new job well.

Telling the family

Sometimes our family and partners have a set view of who we are. They like us like that. They might see that earning a certain amount of money is vital for the smooth running of the household. Without that income they might start to panic. They might like that you work full time and be astonished that you want to work less hours. What will you do with your time? They might be jealous of what you are exploring for yourself. They might not understand the impact health issues are having on you — especially if you are someone who has braved it out so far.

These are all powerful thoughts and emotions, and they are not wrong. This is how your partner or family member feels, so it is worth uncovering and putting to bed, so that those doubts, feelings or thoughts don't get raised on a daily basis as little niggles.

How can I tell them that I want to change?

Be sure to think about this in advance and prepare what you want to say. Consider why you want to make changes. What is the main reason / viewpoint that they will understand?

> *I wanted to reduce my hours, but my husband thought I was good enough to work full time and achieve my potential. He was worried that by stepping back I was going to be sabotaging my career. His desire for me to push myself to the top came from a good place — he saw my potential and wanted me to succeed. However, my health was suffering, and I was missing out on seeing my kids growing up. So, when I sat down to explain to him what I wanted to change, I started with how I felt, how my health was suffering and that I wasn't able to focus on my career right now because I wanted to spend time with the kids. I acknowledged what he was thinking about the future, but I countered it with how I felt now. I also said I could focus on my career later, so I wasn't dismissing his obvious support of me. He heard what I was saying and could understand that this was not forever, it was for now.*

Thinking about things from their point of view

Try to step into their shoes for a minute. Imagine that you are them. Close your eyes if it is helpful.

What *might* they be thinking?

What *might* their main concern at the moment be?

What *might* they be worried about with regard to your suggestion to change roles / career?

Where *might* those worries or concerns coming from?

What *might* be behind the worry?

___

___

___

___

___

Notice these all say 'might' because we can never know unless we have the conversation. However, by thinking about things from their point of view we might get some insights that can help us have a more constructive conversation.

Now think about what you might want to say. Being succinct and clear can be really helpful. Avoid telling a long tale of the past, the whys and wherefores as to why you want to change, and stick to key points.

Avoid putting words into people's mouths. We can make assumptions like, 'You're probably going to say I'm stupid', which might get the conversation off to the wrong start.

Keep it brief and to the point.

What do you want to say?

Why do you want to change?

What will be the benefit to you if you do this?

What will be the benefit to your partner / the family / the household?

What might change, and what needs consideration?

What help do you need?

Make any notes here as you go through the questions.

 **Exercise**

DESC Model

This is a model I use in coaching to help people structure all sorts of conversations at work. I have tailored it to show how you might use it in a more personal conversation like this one.[26]

D – Describe where you are, how work has made you feel, why you want to change

E – Explain the effect it is having on you / the family / your life – give relatable examples

S – State what you would like to do / what you need and what might be worrying you

C – Consequences / Conclude – explain what this means for you – what the benefits are and what you'd like to change with their support

If you are planning on taking a job with a pay cut this will clearly have implications for the household. How will you counteract the shortfall in income? What are you asking to change to enable this to be manageable?

If you are planning on a role with more travel, then there might be less time together or less time for the family. How will this be managed by you all? If you have older children, then consider bringing them into the conversation. How will the change affect them? What support might they be able to give?

> *When I took a contract role, I explained to my children that I wouldn't be able to do as much around the house. They immediately offered to help with the evening meal and other chores.*

A career change might mean better money, but different hours. It might mean more studying. Think about all the angles.

---

26   The DESC script was developed by Sharon and Gordon Bower and is discussed more fully in their book, *Asserting Yourself: A Practical Guide for Positive Change*. DESC stands for Describe, Express, Specify and Consequences.

What changes might be coming if you change roles?

What do you need to cover with your family or partner?

_____
_____
_____
_____

Complete the DESC model template with your ideas:

D — Describe where you are, how work has made you feel, why you want to change

_____
_____
_____

E — Explain the effect it is having on you / the family / your life — give relatable example

_____
_____
_____

S — State what you would like to do / what you need and what might be worrying you

_____
_____
_____

C — Consequences / Conclude — explain what this means for you — what the benefits are and what you'd like to change with their support

---

When do I speak up?

There is no easy answer to this question! All I know is that sometimes sitting down in a formal way seems to be more worrying than just mentioning something in passing — in my household anyway!

I look for times when a conversation is already flowing naturally and then think of a way that I can potentially add in the subject in a 'By the way, I saw a role come up that I really like today' kind of way.

Or if your main reason is health then making sure that your partner is already aware of the concerns you have can make sure that they are pre-warned for the future conversations about role change. 'I felt very stressed today, and it's reinforcing my thinking about looking for something new, but obviously we'd need to give it some thought'. Or 'Today dragged by and it was just so boring and dead-end, I really think it is time for a newer, more exciting challenge... what do you think I am good at?'

Getting them involved so it is a team effort can give your partner or family a real sense of buy-in so that they feel supportive of you and the change you are about to go through.

Talk about the benefits

Sell what you want to your family

Tell them why

What will it mean for you?

For them?

For your household?

Make some notes here as you consider the questions.

_____

_____

_____

Sometimes those benefits might be easily visible — more money, better career, more available hours, better health. But for those that are perhaps more long-term goals then you'll need to explain how the short-term pain, change, or disruption will lead to the longer term benefits all round.

Once you have aired the conversation, other concerns or worries might surface that you have not considered.

Review what has come up and how the conversation went.

Does it change your **ideal job checklist** at all?

Are there amendments to your search criteria that you need to make?

By now you should have a fairly complete **ideal job checklist**, which you *and* your family are happy with.

 # Summary

By now you will have worked out who you might want to share your new plans with, and how they might feel about things, so you are ready to have any necessary conversations.

Take some time to:

1. Consider who you want and need to talk to
2. Think about things from their point of view
3. Use the DESC model to help plan what you might want to say
4. Think about the best time to plan your conversation

Chapter 10

Letting go of the past

IT IS REALLY hard when things have happened to you at work. It can cause huge emotional upset, turmoil and even trauma.

There is a lot that can affect us, and some of the recent upheaval may have formed your reason for searching for a role:

- The highest levels of redundancy ever seen
- High levels of mental health issues
- A pandemic that has changed the way we all work

Knowing that you might have been one of many in the same boat does not lessen the pain and hurt from going through a redundancy process, being unwell or losing a job you loved.

You see that the job market is bouncing back — but the stress of redundancy and the effect on confidence might still be taking its toll.

You know you want to leave a toxic culture, but you might be stressed and anxious about making a move.

You might have been someone on the receiving end of a Settlement Agreement, without the formal redundancy agreement. Also known as the 'tap on the shoulder' with an NDA (Non-Disclosure Agreement), this can sometimes be more upsetting because it is shrouded in secrecy.

A redundancy process is usually an open one and more than one of you are going through it. When you have that 'tap' it can be enormously stressful, not having someone to talk to about it and suddenly having to 'create a reason' for why you are leaving.

When you start thinking about your new job search it can be difficult to overcome pain, anger, and the shock or other emotions when planning for your new role with a sense of distance. Letting go of what has gone before is hard but it is helpful to do so that you can look forward to the new opportunities.

When we get a rejection from work or from a manager it can be devastating. It can knock our self-esteem, our confidence, and our passion for work. Even when we are leaving for positive reasons, it can be hard to let go of our old role, status or teams.

By doing the exercises so far, you have discovered what a more joyful dream job could look like, no matter what the reasons are for doing the search in the first place. You are starting to picture how it might feel to be in a job you really love.

But what if something is still holding you back? It held me back for a while and for many of my coaching clients too. It is worth taking some time now to explore. We will examine how you might be influenced by old patterns and events and look to explore ways to move forward. If you find subject matter crops up for you here that is upsetting or more difficult, don't try to work through it alone; seek advice from a counsellor or GP.

> *It took me ages after I had taken redundancy to feel like I had really got over the rejection. I was in a good job, I was well thought of, I was a top performer. There was nothing I did to cause this; in fact a restructure that I implemented led to me making my own role redundant. In a way, I had done this to myself — for the good of the business. I was well looked after; I had a long notice period — I was asked to hand over the business to the new lead. I left on very good terms.*
>
> *And yet. I still felt rejected. Ashamed. Angry and a bit bitter. I was in effect grieving for my old role and my old team, EVEN though it was the right thing, and I was part of the decision.*

Clients have felt similar:

> *'I was angry. I was bitter. I was lost. I wasn't sure what he was going to do next. All I know is, that it took me a lot longer to get over what had happened, than I gave credit for.'*
>
> *'Ultimately what was holding me back was that sense of anger and disappointment. I've realised through this process that I was still living in the past, retelling my redundancy story,*

and wanting to be heard. I think I thought that by retelling it I would work out why it happened. The thing is, it had happened and now I realise I just need to move on.'

'I had a "tap on the shoulder" and I was devastated. I wanted to get a new job but realised that I needed to deal with what had happened first of all, I felt so let down. My confidence was at an all-time low. I was doubting myself all the time and thinking "Is it me?" I simply couldn't remember what I was good at!'

Many redundancies or lay-offs are immediate, overnight, no-notice affairs and the effect they have on us can be like a crushing blow. You have to pick yourself up — pretty quickly in most cases — and find a new job. When you are feeling at your most bruised, most vulnerable and upset.

The exploration you have done in previous chapters has made you see that you are MORE than just your last job. You are the sum of all your skills and experiences, in life and work, and they will be useful for another organisation out there. You want to get your new job on your terms and get a job you really love in the meantime.

Go back through the earlier exercises, in particular those in Chapter 7 which focus on your skills, talents and passions.

What do those exercises tell you about what you have in your toolbox and what you can deliver to another organisation? Remember what you are good at. Keep reminding yourself daily if you need a boost!

Let's start to reframe the situation you are in now. In fact, this situation may have happened to you years ago, but you might not really have got over it. Many of my coaching clients have left a job and found another one really quickly. Only 18 months or 2 years later do they realise that they are still angry and bitter about the redundancy or job change that happened years before. They then find me and I help them to reset and reframe to get a role they really want!

Get focussed on the future

The past is the past. You can't change it. The business made a decision for whatever reason that didn't include you. It can feel like a kick in the teeth. Everyone has a story about why it shouldn't have been them, and if the manager had only spoken to them sooner, or the management clearly don't know what they are doing.

Yes — possibly all are true, but it is not your problem anymore. You have left. This is now taking up way too much headspace and is getting in the way of you looking for your brand-new dream job.

Worse still, you do not want to be turning up to a new job interview with a grudge, bad blood or a chip on your shoulder that tells other employers that you are a bit of a risk.

So — by doing the exercises in this book you have made a great start. You are thinking about your dream job and what you'd like to be doing.

Learnings from Past Roles / Redundancy

Now let's look at the skills and lessons you learnt from past roles. What can you learn from them that can help shape your decisions?

Questions to consider:

- Do you want to work in a similar sector? Is the challenge facing your old organisation an industry-wide challenge that will just repeat itself? Do you need to retrain or move sector?
- What did the way they handled the redundancy process / communications tell you about the culture? What culture do you prefer if this were to happen again? (In this fast-moving world, roles are likely to be made redundant more often as companies adapt and restructure.)
- What did you learn about yourself? Did you get embroiled in the politics? Were you resistant to change? Did you embrace everything but there just was not a role for you?
- Did you take it personally?
- Could you do with some more training or help in any area?
- What opportunity do you now have that you wouldn't have if you stayed?
- What skills did you learn from that organisation that were of benefit?
- Sometimes we only look at the worst aspect of our employment — that it ended. What did you remember about working there that was good?
- What skills did you learn?
- What people did you meet?
- What connections did you make?
- What technical skills did you learn?
- What soft skills?

- What leadership skills?
- What challenges did you overcome?
- What were your successes?

Instead of thinking of the worst aspects, now is the time to reframe your thinking and think only good things. Can you look again at the decision they made with a fresh pair of eyes? If you were the MD or the shareholders of the business, can you see why they made that decision now? Can you forgive them? And move on? The space that this is occupying in your own thoughts and energy is potentially blocking the good energy that you need to go out and get the job you really want. It's time to put away your hurt, your ego and your pride and think practically and positively about the future.

Now is time to focus on yourself and the opportunity you now have to shape an exact job match and a culture match of somewhere better.

Retelling your story

Sometimes we can get stuck in a loop of telling our 'redundancy' story over and over again. When looking for a new job and thinking about interviews, it is really important to think about the new story you want to tell. Yes, you might feel embittered, angry and resentful. They might have got rid of your role and 'rue the day' that they did. But you now need to move on.

 # Case Study

Marcel

Marcel approached me, three years after his role had been made redundant from a senior sales position. Since then, he had drifted between roles, not really ever finding the level he was at before, not finding the passion. He was feeling quite adrift and was starting to worry as he neared his fifties that he was on the 'scrapheap'.

We did the Slice of Life Exercise. We did the Skill Sets and Finding Your Passion Exercises.

But ultimately what was holding Marcel back was a sense of anger and disappointment. He was still living in the past. He was retelling his redundancy story. He was explaining the whys and wherefores of what had happened and why it should not have happened. He was living his life in the rear-view mirror.

We did an exercise to help Marcel to retell his story.

I asked Marcel, 'What would you like to say to the old organisation / your old manager? Imagine you are talking to them right now.'

Marcel started to speak and was able to say out loud what had been truly bugging him. That he had been told he was next in line. That the next role was his. He was a shoe-in. This was a big shock. How could they have done this to him?

I decided to get him to switch seats. What would his manager say back to him if he heard this?

He considered this. He thought his manager would apologise. Say that he hadn't planned it this way. That he was really good at his job but that there was no room for that role.

I asked him to reflect — how did he feel now his manager was thinking in that way?

He said that he hadn't thought of it that way and could see better the decision that was being made.

I then asked him to change his tack. What would he now say to his manager, three years later, if he was looking at the angle of what he had learnt from that organisation? What skills, attributes and contacts had he taken with him? What was he better off knowing because he had been there?

He started to speak again, reflecting. He was happy he had got so far, that he'd been given various opportunities. That he had great credentials on his CV. That he now had a brilliant network that he could tap into.

What would his manager say to him now, three years on? He thought for a while, and realised that his manager would say 'Why are you doing this role?? You are much more skilled than this. Why are you wasting your talents?'

I asked him to reflect and tell me how he felt now.

He said that he realised he'd been bitter for a long time and that he'd never really addressed what was bugging him. That the exercise had made him consider another point of view (even if it wasn't the true one); he could see the perspective of the business. He could see he had learnt new skills and also that he was pitching the current job search at the wrong level.

What is your new story about why you left?

What will your new future be like?

 **Exercise**

Retelling Your Story

Write down a new 'story' that you can tell when people ask why you left your previous organisation. You aren't trying to tell lies here, but to find a version of the story that you are happier with sharing.

For example:

Bob, the senior manager who was made redundant via a Settlement Agreement because outsourcing had reduced his role.

Version 1

'I really loved my old organisation, to be honest with you, wouldn't have left, but they decided that outsourcing was the way to go, and who am I to argue. Well, I tried arguing but they didn't listen. I doubt it will work; these things go in cycles, don't they? In three years' time it will come back! So my role was struck off and now here I am.'

Version 2

'My role was made redundant when most of my department was outsourced for efficiency reasons.'

Bob is telling the same story but instead of adding his opinions and emotions he remains professional and clear.

What is your version of your story? If it helps, write down what you are currently telling yourself or others (no holds barred) and then try to summarise the distinct facts for a cleaner version 2.

Version 1

Version 2

 **Summary**

Moving forward with positivity is going to be so much better for you than looking back with anger and frustration.

Make sure you have:

1. Considered whether you have anything holding you back
2. Started to think about how you might retell your own story
3. Focussed on the positives and what you gained from various roles and experiences
4. Completed the 'Retelling Your Story' Exercise

Chapter 11

Planning your search

Planning your time wisely

NOW YOU HAVE done the various exercises you can start to make new plans.

No more 'generic' job searches, no more vague titles which mean that you get 300 job alerts in your inbox every day. No more scatter gun applications. Now is the time to take stock and make plans for your new search and your new future.

Time spent now honing your search list will be time well spent. You will only see jobs you want; you will then only read and review opportunities you like, and you'll only apply for what really makes you excited!

We are now planning for your dream job — where you tailor the application and really research the organisation. You only want to do that a few times — because it takes a lot of effort. Planning at this stage will save you a lot of time later.

 **Exercise**

Key Date Planner

Take a moment to reflect on your latest plans:

What dates are relevant to your search now?

_____

_____

_____

_____

_____

_____

_____

Things to consider:

- When do you want a new job by — realistically?
- What dates are you now working to?
- What is your ideal new start date?
- What is your notice period (if any)?
- When will you start your search?
- What dates are you available for interviews?
- When is your first available start date (good to have this in your mind before you start the interview process)?

Procrastination?

Even though you've done all the preparation work, you might still be holding back from taking the next step. If you are making a significant change to your career, hours, location, or grade level, it can feel daunting, and our natural fear response can hold us back from stepping into the 'danger' zone. Take some time to think about what might be stopping you from taking action — because there might be some other thinking that is needed.

Think about what might be holding you back:

Do you feel excited at this next stage or daunted?

Is there something about what you want that is worrying you?

Are you worried you are overqualified or underqualified in an area?

Are you thinking it is too big a move?

What is stopping you from making this step?

What do you need to take action?

What can you do to make yourself take action?

What are you hoping to gain from making this move?

What will motivate you to get on with the tasks?

Why now?

Sometimes it can help to think about how best to set ourselves up for success.

What can you do to make sure you are in the right frame of mind for your search?

Look around your environment; where best can you do the job search? Is it at home? A coffee shop?

When will you take action? Is it first thing before you start work? In your lunch break? Or after work and at weekends? How much time will you be able to realistically commit?

What support do you need from others? Who can proofread your CV or be a sounding board?

What other commitments do you have going on right now that need to be managed around this search?

What else comes up for you?

Is it confidence or fear related? If so — don't worry because we will be looking at how to boost your confidence later on.

Make some notes as you go through the questions — what comes up for you?

_____

_____

_____

_____

Building your portfolio from within – how to feel productive when you are looking

'Getting a job when you have a job is easier,' they say. But what else can you do within that job to boost your CV and skill set with your end goal in mind? If you want to get into leadership / team management roles but there are no opportunities where you are right now, that might be your reason for looking to leave. If you know that your ideal job requires retraining, or a big step change, it can feel like a very big move.

But what can you do now in your current role or situation, to give yourself more of a chance to gain the right skills or create some more interesting examples to say at interview if asked?

Boosting your skills

Things to consider:

Can you get involved with a committee / social / volunteer team?

Can you offer to lead a small project (e.g. fundraising / team days / awareness raising)?

Can you learn about the skill set / topic you need?

Can you take on small extra tasks for your manager? — offer to help do small elements that would help them but also help you and your CV — like planning rotas / organising meetings / creating presentations

What else is your current organisation offering that you could take advantage of? — any online training that is open to all? Health and safety / Mental health first aid / First aid / Mentoring / Coaching training / Technical qualifications / Languages / Driving skills

Talks and networks — can you attend any workshops or talks in a relevant department as a guest? What other upskilling opportunities might they be offering?

Matching your passion — what is your passion area and where do you want to be working? Can you find likeminded people in your current organisation who can help you open up some doors?

Tailoring your search

You can now start to get really specific in your search.

Using your **ideal job checklist** you can start to pinpoint what you want, what type of roles, where they might be and what skills you might be using. You'll also have a better idea of what type of organisation you are looking for. No point in having large global professional firms pop up in your search when you want something smaller and more local.

Take some time to create your search list using your **ideal job checklist** as a guide.

Only add things that you really would want to see in any alert. What sort of ideal organisation would you want to see?

 **Exercise**

Target Companies

Identifying companies

Using the criteria you have noted down, things might start to become clear. Sector, area, location or job role might all start to give you some big clues as to the type of organisation you'd like to work for.

Make a note of any immediately obvious examples of places you'd like to work at or research.

If names of companies are not obvious, you can use your information to identify them. Start talking to friends, family, and colleagues. Read local or regional newspapers, magazines. Do some online searches for companies in that sector. Look at 'Top 100' lists in your sector or area. Use LinkedIn searches to find companies that meet your criteria and follow them, to see what news stories they are posting about.

Once you have an organisation in mind then you can research a little deeper.

Take a look at their website. Do an online search and see what news articles come up – are they positive stories? Do they mention initiatives that you are looking for? Are there any adverse press statements – what are they about? Take a look at online ratings sites such as Reed or Glassdoor; what ranking do they have? Remember that with online ranking sites such as Glassdoor, you'll need to take the scoring and comments with a pinch of salt. It can often be the place where only the disgruntled employees go to vent!

Delete or unsubscribe to any old search criteria / alerts and set up new searches using your new ideal job checklist.

If you are using agencies, give them a call. Tell them that you have been reviewing your requirements.

Tell them what you want and tell them that you won't want to look at those that don't meet those criteria.

You can use the template below to gather your thoughts, or make notes in your notebook.

TARGETING MY SEARCH

KEY INFORMATION
SECTOR, LOCATION, INDUSTRY, SCALE
TARGET COMPANIES I AM INTERESTED IN

MY ONLINE JOB SEARCH APPROACH
AGENCIES, SEARCH ENGINES, LINKEDIN, GROUPS, ALERTS

MY IN-PERSON APPROACH
KEY CONTACTS, PREVIOUS COMPANIES, FRIENDS, FAMILY,
NETWORKING, SECTOR EVENTS

Who do I know?

Once you have identified your search criteria and potential target companies, the next step is to look at who you might know in the sector or organisations.

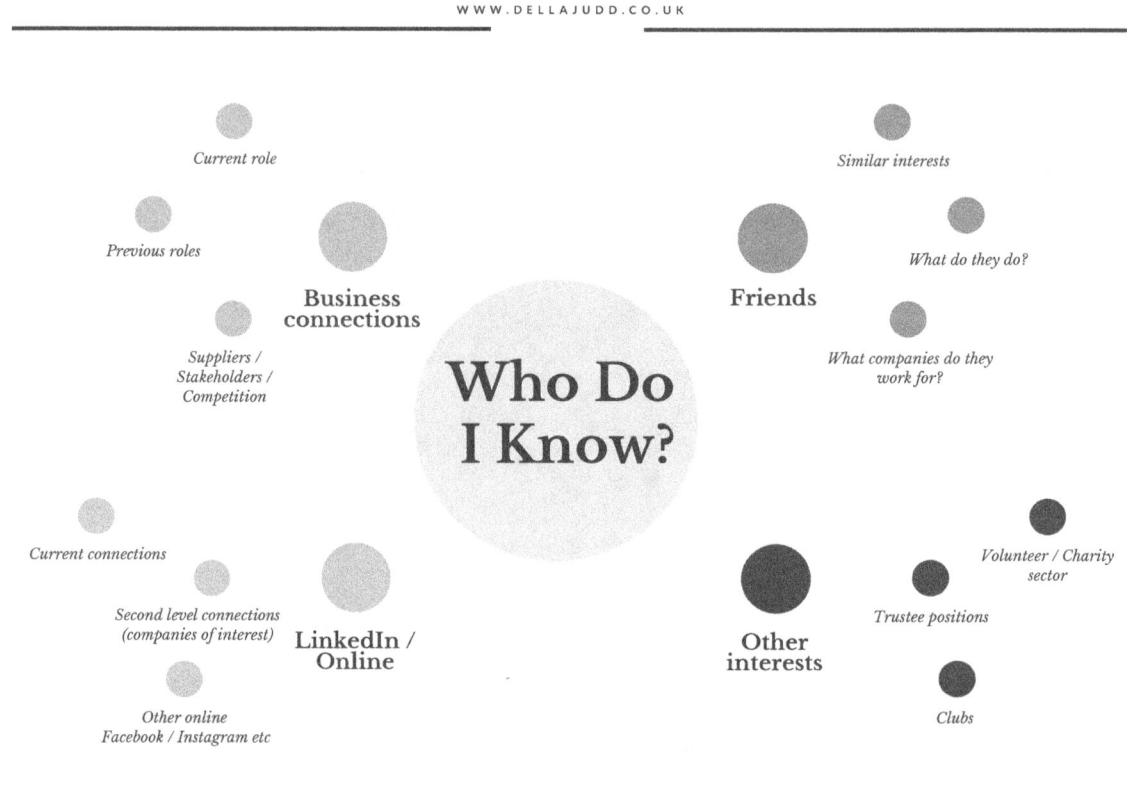

Business connections

Who do you know in the sector? Do you know someone who is already in an organisation of interest? Look within your own organisation, or at people you know within your current organisation — who do they know? What about previous roles — who have you stayed in touch with? Where do they work now?

You might have relationships that you have built up with other companies through your work, such as suppliers, stakeholders or even the competition.

Think about who you know and whether you might be able to have a conversation with anyone.

Don't worry; you are not getting in touch with people to say 'give me a job', you are getting in touch to catch up, to touch base, to find out what it is like working for the organisation, to find out what the culture is like — to start the ball rolling.

If something more comes from the conversation, then great, but if you go in with research and connection in mind, you are likely to relax more and enjoy the process.

If you already have a contact, an organisation or an agency in mind, now is the time to start to make contact.

These early conversations can be very much focussed on fact finding.

Questions to consider when fact finding:

- What is it like to work here?
- What do you love about it?
- Do you think it would suit me?
- What might the challenges be?
- Is there anyone else you think I could / should speak to?
- If I wanted to get into [department] who would be best to meet?

LinkedIn / online search

LinkedIn can be a great tool for finding people that you already know at a target organisation.

Enter the organisation name and up come the first or second connections who work there. If you have a first connection — brilliant.

Consider how you might contact them and ask for a catch-up call, or whether they might answer a few questions via email. Most people are happy to help.

If there is a second connection in common, then consider whether that person can put you in touch with someone they know at the organisation (in an appropriate department). It's a great conversation opener anyway even if they can't put you in touch; you are still talking to people about your search, and they might know someone else.

A great tip is to use LinkedIn to find people who you might want to connect with at the organisation of interest, for example the HR director or sales director. You might be able to follow them, if you can't connect, and see what they are posting about the organisation, which can give valuable insights.

LinkedIn is also great for job alerts and searches, so now is the time to update your profile and search criteria.

You might sometimes get offers to join the LinkedIn 'Premium' service. A coaching client recently signed up for the trial period only which gave them the ability to send people messages directly. It also gave them access to tips on how to find a role, more detailed information on specific roles, as well as high-level candidate profiling which shows a summary of who else is applying for the role. Have a look at what you might get and whether it might suit you.

Delete any old search criteria that you no longer want to see results for. Be ruthless. This is about homing in and only getting notifications for the jobs you actually want to apply for in the first place!

Friends

Sometimes we can overlook friends as a source of information for work, but consider who you know within your circle who is working in a similar way to your own **ideal job checklist**. Our friends also have friends, and partners and colleagues and parents. Those networks can be very fruitful for helping us to meet new people outside of our own circles.

Start by talking in general about what you are looking to change about your life or work. You might be surprised at who knows who!

> *A coaching client who was looking to move into a more senior, but more flexible role, mentioned his new approach at the pub with some friends. They were still in touch with an old mutual colleague from years ago and were able to report that this person was looking for someone for a role that sounded very like what he was describing. They were able to set up a chat and after a few meetings and discussions a new job role was created with him specifically in mind. He had, in effect, created his own ideal job!*

Start talking. Tell people about the work you have done. Tell people that you are looking to move sector, be closer to home. Whatever it is you are most passionate about.

It is amazing what happens when you start talking to people with a passion. People know other people. You never know.

Other interests

If you have interests outside of work such as charity work, being a school governor, volunteering or being part of a gym or club, you will have access to a whole new network that is not currently related to the job you have now.

This is particularly useful for when you have identified that your ideal job is more relevant to those outside interests. If you want to move towards that sector or field, then make sure you are telling everyone and anyone what sort of role you are interested in.

 **Summary**

Make a note of who you might like to speak to and any companies that immediately come to mind that you'd like to research.

1. Business connections you have

2. LinkedIn connections / second connections

3. Friends you can speak to

4. Outside of work people you can mention your search to

Chapter 12

Making the application

YOU HAVE GOT your **ideal job checklist** to hand, you've tailored your searches, you're starting to get back 'out there'. You need a great CV to back you up.

Now is the time to ruthlessly edit your current CV or start from scratch. If you want a very new type or role or want to showcase very different skills then it might be better to start with a blank piece of paper.

Creating a skills-based CV

We are taught to create CVs in a chronological way, with dates showing when we worked and where, often with the job title and location and then a description of the tasks the job involved underneath. There are lots of different ways to create a CV, and if you google it then you'll find lots of (often conflicting) advice. Find an approach that works for you and for the sector you are going into.

My approach is to think of your CV as a way of presenting the skills that you are good at and that you want to show off. You'll still share the dates of the roles, but you'll focus and highlight the key skills and achievements first, creating a summary up front which is what the recruiter sees first.

 # Case Study

Scarlett

Scarlett had been trying to get work for a while and was posting on LinkedIn and Facebook to try and drum up interest. Her sector was going through a very tricky period and there were not many jobs for lots of available candidates.

I met her when she was feeling pretty low. Her CV was OK, but it didn't sing. It was very task based and factual. There was no sense of who Scarlett was.

Before delving into the detail of her CV, I asked her a few general questions.

What do you really want to be doing?

What do you love about the job?

Why do you do it? What gives you the biggest thrill?

What makes you the happiest on a good day?

Suddenly she began to come to life. She talked about helping people, seeing them succeed. Finding good matches and getting brilliant feedback later on. Staying in touch with people and hearing how they did. Hearing from the client about how amazing the candidate was. She was animated, sparkling, happy.

None of that content was in her CV.

We turned to her personal statement. It was a factual list of what her skill set was but with none of the passion or excitement. I asked her to rewrite the statement based on what she had just told me.

She was able to change her statement to say: *'Scarlett is a passionate, experienced and dedicated recruiter, who loves it when great matches happen between candidate and client. She has an open personality which means that she can bring the best out of people and can tune in to the requirements of the client to ensure the best placements.'*

We then turned to other achievements and interests. What else, apart from the task-based activities at work, was she interested in? What had really excited her was her recent involvement in a Mental Health Awareness week where she had been involved on a voluntary basis. She had been part of a team who had organised a week-long series of events. It had got great traction, good feedback, and it had been noticed and appreciated by senior leaders. She wanted to do more of that. To help others.

None of that content was in her CV.

I got her to find a space in the CV for this passion and interest and show how it helped the organisation to improve engagement scores, increase morale and ultimately improve retention rates.

Scarlett went away excited with what she could change about her CV. She had an advert she had seen for an ideal role which she had talked herself out of applying for because she didn't think her CV was good enough. She made the amendments, added the passion and personality, and submitted it. She got an interview the next day and a week later rang me to tell me that she had got a job offer.

She told me, *'I'd forgotten to put my passion and heart into my CV. Once I had done that it made my CV stand out. I then needed to speak confidently at the interview with that level of passion again to get my point across – and it worked!'* She also added, *'Because it was an online interview, I had to practise being confident on my own at home. So, I stood up in front of my camera and pretended I was meeting them face to face!'*

Creating a skills-based CV

Take a look at your CV.

Does it show everything you've done and achieved in the best light?

Is it out of date?

Is it in need of tweaking or a total revamp?

Depending on what your ideal job looks like, you might need to make some significant rewrites.

In Chapter 7 we explored your natural talents and your skill sets. What natural talents do you want to be highlighting in your CV now? Remember this could look completely different to the actual role title you had. You may have done lots of work in past roles that needs highlighting because it doesn't naturally come to mind when looking at a job title. You need your new CV to focus on the elements of work that you want to hunt for now.

You can write multiple CVs for the same job — it's all about the angles.

For example, when I was a customer service director I could have written:

Managed 150 people, controlled a budget of £2.5m and ran large projects.

Firstly, this doesn't highlight enough about me or my skills but if in my DREAM job I want to focus on the people aspect of a role I'd need to dig a little deeper.

I'd need to explore that as well as managing 150 people I:

Set up the first remote / home working team in the company and saw sickness levels reduce

Was responsible for all recruitment, interviews, coaching and mentoring

Set up Mental Health Week and a wellbeing programme for the team

Improved staff engagement scores

The job was the same, but I am delving deeper into other aspects.

If I was looking for a project role I might write that I:

Managed a large restructure and set up the first off-shoring team in India

Dealt with project directors and identified risks, issues and solutions

Did regular reporting with RAG statuses and ROI reports

Same job — different angle.

If I was looking to be in a more commercial / financial role I'd highlight that I:

Saved x amount by outsourcing services

Overhauled the internal budget process to improve time spent on it

Improved expenses reporting and approvals processes

It's all the same job but with a different focus.

Things to consider:

- What do you want to highlight from all your previous work experience?
- What type of role are you looking for?
- Look back at your past experience and assess every job you've had and see what skills and achievements you can pull out from those roles, that reflect where you want to go next.
- Once you've started digging into what you have done / achieved and got skills in, you can then start to focus on what you want to highlight.

An example format:

Opening profile

A description of who you are, what your passions are and what you love to do.

Key achievements — WHAT you have done

- A bullet point list of key achievements you want to highlight
- Show what you personally accomplished or delivered
- Quantify what you have done — some examples to consider:
    - Financially (saved £x by delivering y project)
    - Within timeframes (recruited a new team and got it operational within 3 months)
    - Department wide (led the initiative to implement new systems with x results)
    - For customers (improved services by...)
    - Culturally (increased engagement scores from x to y by doing...)
    - Personally (achieved accreditation in... with [merit / distinction])
    - Changed (radically changed services by...)
    - Business wide (increased sales by x with these initiatives)
    - Values related (assisted in the rollout of social programmes / created a network for minority groups)

Remember, only list achievements that are relevant to your new role and that genuinely highlight your real experience.

Key skills — HOW you do it

- A bullet point list of key skills you want to highlight
- List your natural talents that show how you do what you do
- Add descriptive words
    - Instead of 'coach' you could say 'I am a naturally empathetic and intuitive coach'
    - Instead of 'designer' you could say 'Creative and innovative designer — I speak to many stakeholders to get my inspiration and ensure it links up to the vision'
    - Instead of 'leader' you could say 'Inspiring leader of large teams — I make sure I know people personally, I tell stories to bring the vision to life and I motivate people on an individual basis to get great results'
    - Instead of 'good communicator' you could say 'Excellent communicator — I am always clear, concise and honest and make sure good cascade processes are in place'
    - Instead of 'financial acumen' you could say 'Financially astute — I manage large budgets (£3m) with an eye for detail, I look at the long-term strategy, I write business cases for investment as well as always looking for opportunities to reduce overheads and create efficiency'

Once these key elements are completed then you can start with the work history / experience.

As you go into the list of experience you have had, focus on the skills and achievements you want to highlight, rather than a list of things you were responsible for.

Work history

List the organisation names and dates employed.

List a summary of key responsibilities, achievements, and key tasks (not a long list), anything out of the ordinary (prizes, awards, promotions etc).

Make this new version of your CV about YOU, your skills, your achievements, your passions and much more reflective of the role you are looking for.

CV checklist

If you've found the job you really want, with a culture you really want and it ticks all your boxes, you don't want to fall at this hurdle because of a few silly errors.

Whether you are looking for your first role, looking to move to a new organisation, or looking for an internal promotion or job change, a great CV is what is needed to get you in the door.

Take some time to review and see what you might want to change for yourself. Think of this as a fresh pair of eyes to look at how you approach your CV — small changes that might make a difference.

Tell the truth

This is an obvious one and you might roll your eyes and think OF COURSE. However, I have seen far too many people who TWEAK their job title, EDIT their dates and BOOST their credentials.

Many companies now use screening companies to check that what you state is true. They will check that you did get that degree, you did get those GCSE results, and that you did have that job title, so don't overstate your qualifications or job titles because it may come back to haunt you.

If you have gaps in your CV due to a career break, travelling, parenting, caring etc, it is worth putting that detail in. State what you did between those dates and what you learnt from that life experience. You can still list your achievements and skills.

Reflect language

Consider using the same language or words from the job description in your CV.

Specifically look at the language they use, the types of wording. For example, if they say they want DYNAMIC and you've written ADAPTABLE, you could consider changing it to DYNAMIC. A lot of recruiters use systems to match skills and a computer system might see word matches and pass you to the next stage. If the CV is being manually reviewed, people are busy — but they will unconsciously be noticing word matches and that your CV is talking 'their language'.

Use descriptive language

Some CVs can read just like a list of tasks, job roles, systems, and numbers. It can be really difficult as a reader to get any sense of the person who wrote the CV without using some more descriptive language. Using energetic language can really get a sense of what you are really like to work with too, important for getting a good cultural fit. Equally, if you are applying for a specialist role, then using the appropriate technical language would be more appropriate.

Here are some examples:

Describing tasks:

I create *compelling* content.
I *actively* look for opportunities for process improvement.
I *fastidiously* check for errors when proof reading, with a real eye for detail.
I love creating *absorbing* and *engaging* presentations that *captivate* my audience.
I am *detail-orientated* and *patient* which is essential in this field.

Describing yourself:

I am *passionate* about making improvements within the diversity and inclusion agenda.
I get *excited* about delivering excellent customer service.
I get great *satisfaction* when I see people in my team develop.
I *enthusiastically* tackle tasks.
I am a *considered* decision maker who weighs up pros and cons.
I *love* to *innovate* and suggest new ideas.

NB: Always make sure you remember to describe your skills and achievements in line with the first point – 'tell the truth'. This is about sticking to the facts and making sure you highlight them in the best possible light.

Personalise applications

Sending out a blanket CV means that you may have lost the opportunity to tailor the language and the ability to re-order the key skills and achievements to show the best match for the role.

It does take time to personalise each CV or application – whether that is online, via video or via an agency. However, you are only applying for jobs you really want, so you can take a little more time to make sure that they are tailored and hitting all the right marks.

- Make your application show how you are relevant; adjust any ordering of skills and achievements to put the most relevant at the top.
- Review the key phrases and words that they are using and tweak any to get a good match.
- Review the organisation's website and, if relevant, add any additional information.
- If a covering letter or summary is called for, then add to the application why you would like to work for them specifically. Make this personal, not just a copy and paste from a previous application.

Save all the versions of the CVs you do, adding the organisation name to the document name, so you can find it again when you go to the interview. You can also save specific text that you've used for covering letters for reference or to use again.

Spell check, grammar, fonts and format

Please don't fall at the final hurdle with a typo or spelling mistake!

Print off the CV and read it out loud. This sounds basic, but the brain will see or hear errors when reading out loud that it has missed when you were scanning a screen.

A CV riddled with errors is the first route to an easy rejection.

Avoid using weird fonts and fancy layouts. While these look good they sometimes cannot be read by the automated tools that many companies and agencies now use. It means that keywords are harder to pick up and your CV might not make the cut.

Check what format you are required to send your CV in. Often we think PDF is a good format but many companies still want to see a CV in Word format.

Google yourself

Now let's assume you've wowed them with your CV — it was tailored, personalised and it left them energised and wanting more. What do you think they might do next? A lot of hiring managers and recruiters will then go online and see what they can find out about you. Ideally they are finding a very professional LinkedIn profile and some good news stories. But what else might they find?

Have you ever googled yourself?

If you haven't googled yourself — do it now!

Have a look at what comes up. Are you happy that your photos / your comments / your holiday in Ibiza come up?

Are you happy that a potential employer might see them?

If not, consider changing your privacy settings to be visible to just your nearest and dearest.

With many people applying for roles you don't need to give people any excuse to turn you down!

Beyond the CV – other stages

Cover letters

Never underestimate the power of a cover letter. Despite all of the technology we now have at our fingertips, many organisations are still looking for cover letters, and a great one can really open doors. Create a tailored cover letter for each role and if you do use 'cut and paste' for some of the text, be sure to check that you have changed the organisation name, job title or other key information. If you don't then that is a sure-fire way to get yourself filtered out! As an HR manager told me, 'I've seen many cover letters that have been submitted for the wrong role or have not been proofread to ensure that they are relevant to the application!'

Take a look at online resources for more guidance and tips.

Online applications

These days you can get asked for all sorts of different supporting information as you make your application. You might be asked to apply in new ways using technology.

Some considerations for online applications, tests and video:

- Make sure you've applied in the right format and have done all the steps they have asked for.
- Practise in front of a camera if you have to do an online application.
- Understand exactly how much time you have.
- Make sure you have rehearsed your key points if you can see the questions in advance. If you can't, make sure you have thought about the sort of thing that will come up and rehearse your own opening introduction.

- Read any examples that they provide in advance.
- Take any practice time that they give you, and re-record if you can if you feel you need to.
- Make sure you can be heard properly and test your microphone before starting.
- Test your lighting set-up — can people see your face?
- Check what is behind you; do people need to see your washing up? Consider using a professional virtual background (not an image of the beach or a personal photo), or blurring the background.
- Check how you are sitting; consider your posture and how you will come across, just as you would in a face-to-face interview.

Update your LinkedIn profile with relevant information

When you have submitted your CV, the recruiter is likely to search for you on LinkedIn. A lot of people use LinkedIn now to create their own personal brand profile, which can showcase you, your work history and your interests. It can be a great way to show your passions, values and skills as well as focus on the role and organisation you might be looking for.

Things to consider:

What would they find there?

Does your profile match the CV? With the same dates and companies?

What does your profile say about you?

Is your profile showing a picture of 10 years ago?

What extra information can you put on your profile that you can't put on your CV?

- Any certificates / qualifications?
- Any testimonials?
- Any pictures of you at events, winning awards, taking part in a charity day?

What can you do to make yourself look appealing to recruiters?

Does LinkedIn reflect your values and where you want to be going?

If you are looking to jump sector, start to follow companies that are relevant to you to see what trends are happening in that area; what are they posting about?

Can you post, like or share some articles that are relevant? People will start to see what you are interested in.

Take a look at what is on your profile — edit anything that is old or out of date. Consider deleting anything that might detract from your new search.

Apply wisely

Finally, make sure that you apply only for the roles that you can see yourself doing.

If a job comes up and on closer inspection it states a particular requirement, if it is on your drop-dead non-negotiable list, then don't even bother.

If it is very close in all other aspects, it might be worth calling the agency or recruiter to ask whether that is a firm criterion or whether there is some flexibility.

Ask agencies about salary and the organisation. They can be a bit secretive but how do you know if you want to work there if you don't know the organisation name?

Make a shortlist of any good opportunities.

Read and then re-read the requirements.

Does the role and organisation match your **ideal job checklist?**

Once you are happy that it is a great match, tailor your application and hit SEND!

 **Exercise**

Key Date Planner

Applications are now being sent and you will start to hear back for interviews soon, so take a few moments to think about next steps.

What dates are relevant to your search now?

___

___

___

___

___

___

___

Things to consider:

- What dates are you now working to?
- What is your ideal new start date?
- What is your notice period (if any)?
- What dates are you available for interviews?
- When is your first available start date (it's good to have this in your mind before you start the interview process)?
- When will you do your interview preparations?

 **Summary**

Having a great CV can make all the difference.

Make sure you have:

1. Considered rewriting your CV from scratch if needed
2. Looked at making a skills-based CV
3. Reviewed the CV checklist
4. Updated your searches
5. Applied only for things you really want!

Chapter 13

Feeling confident – before, during and after

CONFIDENCE IS KEY to putting yourself forward and presenting your best self. It's why I wanted to dedicate a whole chapter to it. Because if you've found what you really want to be doing, you want to make sure you feel confident enough to go out and get it.

Imposter syndrome

Even now, after years of living and years of working, the old imposter in me can still raise her ugly head. And as a coach, I often see skilled, senior, experienced people struggling with confidence. It is something I would say that every one of us experiences at some point. That feeling of dread, of nervousness, the fear of being 'found out', the constant comparison to others. Men can experience it just as much as women and it can really hold you back. One recent study[27] showed that 75% of women had experienced imposter syndrome at some point in their career and it is estimated that 20–30% of all high achievers have experienced it. (And the rest are lying!!)

---

27 KPMG study finds 75% of female executives across industries have experienced imposter syndrome in their careers, KPMG US, https://info.kpmg.us/news-perspectives/people-culture/kpmg-study-finds-most-female-executives-experience-imposter-syndrome.html#:~:text=Key%20findings%20of%20the%20study,by%20women%20in%20corporate%20America

It is why working on our confidence and self-belief is just as important as working on the job application process itself.

You have to believe what you are saying, you have to sell yourself and you have to let yourself speak with real confidence.

What can low confidence mean if you are job hunting?

It can mean you are afraid to look for a role at the right level.
It can mean you are underselling yourself when it comes to skills.
It can mean you are taking less of a package than you deserve.
It can mean you don't even apply to the dream job because you don't think you deserve it.
It can mean you look at poor companies or poor culture and settle for something less than brilliant.
It can mean that you are fearful when you start a new role.
It can mean that you are nervous in interview and so don't get the dream role.

So, it means we need to sort it out!

Here's what we will do:

We will look at how you can start keeping track of your good points.
We will look at how you can build your confidence on a daily basis.
We will look at how you start to believe in yourself.

If you don't believe you are worthy of the role you have now, or think you have got there by luck, then you will not be likely to present your best self when looking for a new role.

Have you ever felt any of the following:

- You got there by luck?
- You will be found out?
- You are winging it?
- You are making it up as you go along?
- Someone will question who are you to be doing this job anyway?
- Someday this will all be taken away?

If so, you are not alone. Nearly everyone has felt this way.

Let's start building our own confidence up!

'I am not qualified'

When we are assessing the job advert it's important that we can recognise the skills that we have and how they can match. As well as understanding what we ARE good at (which we covered in the 'Skill sets and natural talents' section), we need to feel confident in saying that we are good at them.

A Hewlett-Packard study showed that men will apply for a job if they match 60% of the criteria in a job specification, whereas women will only apply if they match 100%.[28] It means that most women and some men are potentially better qualified for a role but that they don't even apply for it. What a crying shame!

We can all be better at identifying and acknowledging our skills and assessing how qualified we are to do a role.

Instead of looking at job specification criteria and thinking 'Well I never had that in any of my previous job descriptions', think again.

Assessing job descriptions

Here's an exercise in reassessing the words and language used to describe certain experience or tasks.

Job specification criteria:

- Strategic
- Visionary

People have often said to me that they are not 'strategic' or 'visionary' because they are comparing themselves to a very public entrepreneur figure, or the most senior director in their organisation. You don't need to be Richard Branson or Elon Musk to be visionary.

Think about what that word means, literally.

---

28   Why Women Don't Apply for Jobs Unless They're 100% Qualified, Harvard Business Review, https://hbr.org/2014/08/why-women-dont-apply-for-jobs-unless-theyre-100-qualified

Look at the grade they are recruiting for — a visionary team leader will be different to a visionary director.

What is the organisation looking for?

What might they mean by it? What might it mean within that role or department?

Let's break it down:

Strategic — *Thinking outside the box, considering the competition, assessing the wider vision, looking at different angles. Being a clear thinker, having a plan. Being calculated and deliberate in your thinking.*

What in your life could you demonstrate in that area — even if it was not in any of your previous job descriptions? Where in your previous jobs have you done something in one of those areas?

Here are some ideas:

- I came up with new ideas or new ways to tackle a problem
- I noticed that the competition were doing something and I looked at how we could respond
- I keep up with trade magazines and industry changes
- I implement the wider vision and look for ways to bring that strategy to life for my teams. I show my team where they fit into the vision
- I always think ahead and make plans (work and home)
- I know when the budget planning process is, so I can do my research up front and plan for new projects and initiatives
- I know who to speak to when something needs doing or when it goes wrong
- I have long-term plans at home about how we will pay off our mortgage
- I always look at new ways to tackle challenges, in fact I moved house twice to be nearer to my parents
- I took my exams in CIPD so that I could move into this sector; I knew it would take me years but I had a long-term plan

Visionary — *Has a clear vision of the future. Has ideas. Is creative. Plans for the future. Is inventive. Can see long into the future. Can imagine new ways of working.*

What in your life could you demonstrate in that area — even if it was not in any of your previous job descriptions? Where in your previous jobs have you done something in one of those ways?

Here are some ideas:

- I set long-term goals. I create the goals and can see where we want to take this team and department
- I look at new ways of doing things. I often overhaul processes and procedures to ensure that we are doing them in the best way possible
- I believe in continuous service improvement
- I implemented an ideas log for the team
- I ask my team what is going on so we can always improve
- I speak to customers about what they want and what they need
- I look at the future of technology
- I keep up to date with trends and news to ensure that I am ahead of the curve
- I attend webinars and listen to great speakers
- I plan long term ahead for my family and my life
- I am always the one thinking of new ideas for the house
- I am the one who can see new ways of tackling a domestic issue
- I had to think outside the box when my mum took ill during Covid
- I had to get creative when home-schooling my two youngsters

Here are two more short examples:

- Self-starter
- Well organised

Self-starter — *a person who is sufficiently motivated or ambitious to work on their own initiative without needing direction. Gets things done.*

What in your life could you demonstrate in that area — even if it was not in a working environment?

- I plan ahead and make plans for holidays / trips / schools
- I am always looking at what I can learn next
- I have signed up to self-study
- I am always looking at work as to what else I can do
- I take it upon myself to improve systems
- I can see when things need attention and just get on with it

Well organised — *a person who is structured, well planned, clear, defined and efficient.*

What in your life could you demonstrate in that area — even if it was not in a working environment?

- I manage a household of five people
- I organise all the caring / shopping / laundry
- I created an online filing system which improved time to find things
- I plan my diary and those around me
- I make sure I can re-use content for more than one purpose

These lists are just examples. But it shows that no matter what level of role you have you can look for areas where you are doing more than you think you are. Take a look at any areas that you feel underqualified for in a job description and think about what other ways you could look at your own experience to enhance your CV.

# Exercise

Job Description Review

Write down each word in a job description that is currently appealing to you, but maybe you are feeling a little bit afraid to apply for. Break down each section and write down the keywords.

_____

_____

_____

_____

For each keyword look at what that wider meaning could be. Look at what that could mean for the role you are applying for. Look at the definition in the dictionary if it helps. Look at the role, the department and the grade. What is realistic at that level?

_____

_____

_____

Then sit and think about where in your roles — present and past — you could show even a small element of that skill or experience.

_____

_____

_____

_____

_____

_____

Then think about how you could show that skill from your home life.

_____

_____

_____

_____

_____

_____

Start practising doing this for each job role and application.

If when you have done the exercise, you are still finding gaps where you feel that you cannot demonstrate enough experience comfortably, then it may not be the job for you. And that is fine. Only apply for jobs that are the best fit.

Remember your successes

Not many of us can remember what we are good at. Not many of us really know what our natural talents are. And hardly any of us record and capture what we are good at. Wouldn't it be great to tap into what it felt like when we did something good? Here's an example of an exercise I did with a coaching client and one you can do yourself too.

 **Case Study**

Melanie

Melanie was feeling particularly low when I met her for coaching. Despite being a senior HR director, she had got to such a low point that she had simply forgotten her own abilities and achievements. A recent bout of structure changes, low-level bullying and an overbearing manager had made her doubt herself. Firstly, I got her to close her eyes and remember a time when she had been successful. She shut her eyes and started to remember. I asked her to remember the place, where she was, what she was doing, what she could see. I asked her to remember what she was saying, how she was standing. I prompted her to think about how she felt, what was she wearing, what was her posture like, where were her feet and her hands?

After she had spent some time in that 'zone', I asked Melanie to recall what she had noticed. She said that she could remember a time at her previous organisation where she had to take charge in a crisis. That the issue had been challenging, but she had taken charge. She had dealt with a very difficult person and had been strong and determined. She felt in control and centred. She noticed that she was standing in front of a team presenting, standing tall, with her feet firmly planted and her posture was upright and 'strong'. She was wearing 'kick-ass' heels and a good suit — not a brand new one but one she knew made her look good and felt comfortable at the same time. Her breathing was steady and whilst she felt adrenalin flowing it was 'in a good way'; she felt 'buzzed'.

She started to remember who she was before this recent bout of challenges, and could piece together more of her skills, attributes, and qualities when she was in that positive, confident mindset.

We then started to review other skills and experiences, so that Melanie had a great list that would start to build her CV and her confidence. She suddenly said: 'I am good at what I do, I'd just forgotten!'

Melanie started to build her CV and worked on her interview technique. She often used the visualisation technique to get herself back into the positive mindset.

Exercise

Remembering Your Successes

A good first step is to remember what you are good at. You can start by doing the visualisation that Melanie did in the case study above. The wording for it is below. Take some time to read it or you can record yourself reading it out (take care to add spaces for thinking time) and then listen again. You can download the recording on my website / free resources link.

Make notes in the space below after you have done it to capture everything:

Take some time to relax, take a few deep breaths.

Go back in time to a moment when you felt really confident.

Really tune in to that moment. Take a few seconds to remember.

We are going to dig into what it was about that event that made you feel confident. What can we learn from it for our interview preparations, for our new job and indeed, for our life?

So, you've got your memory of when you felt really confident.

Where are you? What can you see?

What does it feel like?

What can you notice from the experience?

What do you notice about your body? How are you sitting or standing?

What is your posture like? What about your breathing? Where is your head? And your hands? What is going on with your feet? What about your face? Your mouth?

What is the situation you are in? What are you doing that makes you feel so confident?

Who is with you? Are you alone? Are you with others?

What are you wearing?

Is there anything you notice about what you are wearing that gives you confidence?

When was this memory? What does the memory tell you about confidence?

What would you need to do now to make you feel that confident again?

Take some time after reliving that memory to make any notes about what you noticed.

_____

_____

_____

_____

_____

_____

_____

Is there anything from that reflection exercise that could help you?

_____

_____

_____

_____

_____

Capturing compliments

Remember the Natural Talents Exercise in Chapter 7?

That can be a great place to start when thinking about building up your confidence.

Go back and look at what you captured.

What were your key talents?

What were the areas where people complimented you?

It can be helpful to start a log of compliments, where people said 'Thank you' or 'Well done', note down any comments where people said 'I couldn't have done this without you' or 'That was so helpful' — write it all down.

Think of this as your 'compliment bucket'.

Even the smallest compliment or bit of praise can be useful for you to top up your own bucket. With practice you can keep popping in the little comments or the big bits of praise so that you always feel that you have a bucket of positivity to carry around with you. You can use the template below to start filling in your compliments.

 # Exercise

Compliments List

Compliments	Praise / Rewards	Performance review feedback

Keeping track can help to boost you.

Take a look at it before writing your CV, making an application or doing an interview.

How did you do it?

As well as praise, it can be helpful to think about your achievements. Not just WHAT you delivered, but HOW you made a difference. What did you specifically do to get it done? What was it about you and your personality / skills / approach that got it done?

How I did it:

There is a difference between noting down WHAT you delivered and recognising what YOU did to make it happen.

Here's an example from my days as a customer services director:

My achievement:

Service desk achieving 'world class' status from a benchmarking company

How did it get done?

A large number of initiatives:
Benchmarking
Training
Technical improvements
Staff motivations
Positive recognition
New technology

What did I do specifically?

I got the business case signed off and sold the need for benchmarking
I set goals for managers and kept track of progress
I took an interest in the people and praised them when change happened
I developed a culture of success and recognition
I persuaded the department head that investment was needed in new technology

What was about me and my personality?

I had the vision to see where we wanted to go and what good customer service looked like
I was good at articulating the vision to my team, standing up in front of them and delivering interesting and engaging presentations
I engaged the team in workshops to help them work out the solutions, to get buy-in
I had energy, enthusiasm, and drive, even on bad days
I persevered and made sure to follow up — lobbying for what I wanted
I took a lot of time to escalate issues, persuade leadership and train my team
I was able to present a compelling business case, using influencing skills to sell all the benefits

Do you see the difference between saying:

'I got the service desk to achieve world class status by implementing new technology and training my team'

To being able to say:

'I had a vision to get the team to world class status; I got the business case approved for the funding to do benchmarking, and then motivated and engaged the team and the managers to drive the project forward. Once the project was live, I kept the energy and interest going and was constantly looking at how I could help solve problems and praise the progress.'

Take some time to look at your CV to ensure that you are highlighting what you did, how you did it and what it was about you and your personality that made things happen.

Confident interviews

You're running late. You forgot to find out where to park. You've been driving round in circles, and you've only just found a space. You have a longer walk than you'd like, and you arrive at reception feeling a bit hot and sweaty and totally flustered.

I feel anxious just reading that back! How does it make you feel? Do you feel calm, in control and ready to face an interview?

You leave the house 20 minutes earlier than you need, so that you can make sure that you get a parking space in front of the building. When you get there, they are all taken, but no matter, you know there is another car park next door. You head there, find a space, buy your ticket, and walk towards the office building. You're 20 minutes early, so you ask the receptionist if you can use their facilities to freshen up. Once done, you take a seat in reception and wait for your interviewer.

Feel better? I do too! It always amazes me how many people turn up to interviews red faced, out of breath and with their mind on the parking or the traffic. Make sure that you are in the calm camp when it comes to interviews.

A study by Amy Cuddy[29] shows that our body language can affect how we feel. If we feel flustered and fearful (of not finding a space, or of the interview itself) our hormones react accordingly, with testosterone, our bravery hormone, falling and cortisol, our stress hormone, rising. Conversely, she found that if we felt calm and powerful then the reverse happened: testosterone rose and cortisol fell.

It's not just about what happens before we arrive at the interview, but what posture we choose whilst we are waiting.

If you arrive at the interview and slump over your phone or jiggle your legs nervously, you're putting yourself into a 'low-power' position where the stress hormones kick in and bravery ones go down.

If we put ourselves into a 'high-power' position such as standing tall with our feet shoulder width apart then the opposite happens: the testosterone goes up and the cortisol down. Amy calls it the power pose, and her studies show that standing up in the 'Wonder Woman' pose for just two minutes can change our hormones and physically make us more confident.

So, planning ahead and arriving early not only gives you a chance to go to the bathroom and freshen up, but it also gives you the chance to stand in a power pose for two minutes and correct your hormones. You can also read your notes and remind yourself of your key skills and achievements. Plus, you look professional because you have arrived on time.

Online interviews can be a minefield too. Do the same for an online interview as you would with a face-to-face one. Give yourself time and space between what you were doing before and the interview. Don't just jump from one call to the interview. Create some space, read your notes, do the power pose and sit calmly waiting before the allotted time for the call.

---

29 Your body language may shape who you are, Amy Cuddy, YouTube, https://www.youtube.com/watch?v=Ks-_Mh1QhMc

Managing your emotions

Did you know that butterflies in the tummy can be interpreted as nerves and fear, as well as excitement and anticipation? The difference is often down to what we tell ourselves about the situation. Usain Bolt, when he stood at the start of the 100m race, experienced those feelings and he recognised them as positive energy that was going to power him across the line.

A coaching client I was working with recently felt a constant sense of fear every time their manager messaged them to say, 'Can we speak?' Immediately, my client experienced a tightening of the stomach, a dry mouth, and a sense of rising panic. It was starting to affect their everyday moods. Often once the call had taken place, they realised that there had been nothing to worry about; their manager had simply had a question or was passing on a piece of information. We needed to work on the perception that the 'can we speak' message meant doom! We did the following exercise to help them reframe.

 **Exercise**

Reframing Your Emotions

Think of a scenario that makes you feel physically nervous or anxious. Perhaps it is related to your job search, perhaps not. For this exercise I will use the example of being nervous for a job interview.

How I feel	How I want to feel
Nervous	Excited
Fearful	Curious
Anxious	At peace
Sick	Calm
Panicky	Still

Now you have identified some different ways of feeling about the same scenario, you can start to practise setting an intention to feel a different way.

When I did the exercise with my client, they realised that they had started to develop a repeating pattern around their manager and the message, 'Can we speak?' They decided that in reality they had no idea of what they were going to say, so should not try to predict it. Instead, they decided to mentally think, 'I wonder want they want' every time that message came up. By deciding to be curious on each occasion they went into the conversation much more calmly. And, as in most cases, the conversation was nothing to worry about.

What repeating patterns are you creating around your job search?

Make a note in the template and think about how you could change it around to be feeling something different instead. Think about how you feel when these situations happen.

Example symptoms / signs:

Sweaty palms, sick, butterflies, tics, headaches, muscle ache, shaking, anger, upset, fear, anxiety, worry, confusion, impatience, irritation, nauseous

How I feel	How I want to feel

Once you have found an 'alternative' way of thinking or feeling then you can start to practise it.

In our example, replacing fear and nerves with curiosity meant that my client made a decision to notice each time the message 'Can we speak?' arrived. When it arrived, they took some deep breaths and said to themselves 'I wonder what they want' and 'I don't know what they want; until I do I will be curious'. They even made a note that sat by their desk reminding them that when nerves happened they would replace the feeling with 'calm' or 'curious' actions.

 # Summary

Once you start to put all of these confidence-boosting tips into practice, you'll be ready for anything! Make sure you've gone through the actions to:

1. Reframe how you assess language in job adverts
2. Remember your successes
3. Capture compliments
4. Look at not WHAT you do but HOW you do it
5. Take time to prepare — for interviews and for giving your responses
6. Practise the power pose
7. Reframe your emotions

Chapter 14

Getting the role / Interviews

SO, YOU HAVE identified the companies, done the research, tailored your CV, applied for the job, and now you have an interview.

The good thing is that because you have done all the prep and identified only the jobs you REALLY want, you genuinely will be approaching the interview with excitement and a sense of purpose. You want this job, you like the organisation and the culture; it matches your values and your vision of where you see yourself.

This makes the language you use and the preparation easier because you will be speaking from the heart.

 **Exercise**

Checking In

CHECKPOINT — Does that all ring true with this job?

Do you really want it?

If you were offered the job today, would you take it?

If not — what is coming up for you?

_____

_____

_____

_____

Take some time to just sit with these questions. Sit for 5 or 10 minutes or go for a walk. Contemplate the reality of getting THIS particular job.

Is it really what you want?

Can you see yourself working there happily?

Does it match your **ideal job checklist**?

If there are any doubts coming up — focus on those.

What comes up?

Where can you feel it in your body? Is it in your head, chest, stomach?

What emotions are you feeling right now?

What is underneath those emotions?

What is your body telling you?

_____

_____

_____

_____

*I recently turned down a contract because it didn't **feel** right. What do I mean by that?*

Well, I have realised that when work or jobs don't feel right my body starts to complain and my emotions feel off. I have to really tune in to the feelings and I have to listen to them. On the day of a meeting about a contract, I woke up feeling miserable, my head was aching, and I just felt so low. There was no other reason; I was just back from a holiday, and I felt well, healthy and relaxed. But emotionally, I just felt like lead.

I sat and listened to what my emotions were saying to me. Ultimately the piece of work, whilst on paper it looked ok, the set-up of the contract, the type of work, the money, the time it would take up, all felt slightly wrong. I chatted it over with my partner and speaking it out loud helped me to articulate that I just wasn't feeling right about it. I could already feel the stress starting to pervade my body and I knew that if I started the work and carried on that the stress would grow, and my health would suffer. So I stopped, politely called the person and declined the work.

As soon as I did that I felt something in me lift. A weight was off my shoulders and suddenly I felt energised to do something else. I felt that I could turn to another piece of work and give that work, where my passion lies, my energy and my effort.

How does *your* body feel when you think about this new work?

_____
_____
_____
_____

Who could you chat things over with?

_____
_____
_____
_____

Would speaking out loud to yourself help? Or a good friend, a coach?

_____

_____

_____

If you picture yourself in the role in three months' time, how can you imagine you will be feeling?

_____

_____

_____

_____

_____

_____

_____

_____

If you can do this exercise and still feel excited and buoyant about the job, then the chances are you have found a good match. If there are any doubts, explore them and see what they are.

If it is a good match and you still feel excited and keen, then we can turn to the interview preparation.

Interview top tips

You've now been invited for an interview — congratulations!

Preparation is essential but make sure you are working on the right things!

Start by feeling confident — now is not the time for the shy or reticent version of you to appear. Revisit the previous chapter about confidence and do any of the exercises that you might find helpful before the event.

A few tips:

Be on time — Whether it's online or face to face. Make sure you have done your planning, know where to park or have downloaded and tested the relevant online meeting tools.

Dress confidently and appropriately — Not everyone is going to expect a suit and tie nowadays, but it can feel good to wear something appropriate for the sector or the role you are going for. A marketing creative will likely wear something quite different to a senior executive for a bank. Feel good in yourself; be smart and clean and tidy. There are still a lot of different views about dress code with some people very much in the 'be yourself' camp whilst others still expect a more 'traditional' view. I would recommend you do your research but ultimately it is about feeling comfortable so that you can be your best in the interview.

Know the business — You will have already done some research into the organisation before you applied for the role. It's worth doing more preparation for the interview, especially thinking about the specific department and the challenges they might be facing. Don't underestimate the value of this; it might be the difference between candidates. I am always amazed by the number of candidates who have done little or no research.

Answer the questions! — This might sound obvious, but you'd be surprised at how many people don't stick to the point or have done no preparation for the most obvious starter questions. Be succinct and brief — don't waffle on; answer them and then be quiet, and wait for the next one. Remember what the interviewer wants to hear is how it is relevant to THIS job.

Example starter questions:

- *Give me a run-through of your career / CV to date:*
    - Keep it brief — start with the latest job and only mention what is relevant to this role. (Not a full history which goes back decades!)

- *Why are you interested in this job? What particularly interests you about working for this organisation?*
    — Do your research and be genuine.

- *What key skills would you be bringing to the organisation?*
    — Remind yourself of the key skills you highlighted in your CV and make sure you are prepared with the most relevant ones for the role.

Ask a good question — The interviewer wants to see engagement; they want to see your interest in the organisation. The more senior the role the more essential this is. There has been many a time when, as an interviewer, I have got to the end of an interview and asked, 'Have you got any questions for us?' and had the reply, 'No, I think that's everything'. Really? How can you know everything without asking a question!

Questions at the end do make a difference.

I was hiring for a team manager role and the candidates were all in a similar position and gave similar answers, so the ONLY deciding factor was the question at the end. The stand-out candidate asked about my vision for the team and for the future. They used it as a way of getting some insights into my head, which if they got the job (and they did) would mean they would be better equipped.

Questions to avoid:

- When will I hear?
- How much holiday do I get?
- How much sick pay do I get?

Questions to consider:

Ask the interviewer:

- What is the ultimate vision you have for the organisation / department / team?
- What is the strategic direction for the next few years?
- What do you love about working here?
- How have you progressed here; what has been your greatest success?
- How do the people in the team feel about the changes / restructure (where relevant)?
- What do you think the biggest challenges for this role / department will be?
- What opportunities are there for mentoring others?
- How much focus is there on training and development?

- Where do you see the team in three years' time?
- If I was successful, where do you see I could make the biggest impact?
- What is the thing that needs resolving first?
- How would you describe the culture of the organisation / team?
- What key initiatives is the organisation looking to implement at a high level? (If you are interested in corporate social responsibility / green / diversity then you can angle the question towards that)
- Do you have a Diversity and Inclusion network that I could get involved in?
- I love doing charity work; is there a way for me to get involved?

Stay calm — Practise breathing techniques, do your power pose and look at your body language, making sure you are holding yourself in a confident and open manner. The person doing the interview may well be nervous too — this might be their first time, so remember they are just a human being too! (This makes them a lot less scary.)

Remember the passion — Remember why you want this particular job and what you put into your CV about why you wanted it. Make sure this is reflected in the interview preparation.

Interview extras

Sometimes you will be asked to prepare a presentation for the interview, depending on the role.

Some things to consider:

- Answer the question or respond to the statement asked.

- What do you think they WANT to hear?

- Why might they be asking?

- Don't just tell them everything you know on the subject! No matter how extensive that knowledge is, keep it relevant and to the point.

- Think about the style of presentation and what technology will be available to you, if any. Do you need a PowerPoint deck? If you do create a presentation, keep it high level with very few words on the slides.

- Have a back-up – in case the technology fails, have a printout ready if you are meeting face to face. Test the sharing functionality of the meeting software to ensure you are familiar, if online. Consider sending a copy via email in advance in case of difficulty.

- Be yourself, be natural – remember they want to hear from you, your views and your style. Do whatever you need to do to be as relaxed as possible. Remember to laugh and smile! A sense of humour can be a real help.

- Speak without notes – if you can. We speak much more naturally without notes. Notes can make everything sound slow and stilted. You know your subject; trust yourself.

- Passion – remember to inject it into your presentation. Show some energy and enthusiasm.

- Rehearse and practise – try saying the words out loud. Preparing in your head or on paper is not the same as speaking. Find a quiet spot and deliver the talk out loud to yourself. Recording it can be helpful because we sometimes say things very differently when we speak. Having a recording can give us those nuggets of information so we can build them into the presentation and remember them for next time!

Creating your stories

I remember getting ready for my Director Assessment Centre day at Deloitte. Part of the day was to have an interview with two senior partners. I asked a friend and colleague to help me with the prep. I turned up to her house with a large A4 notebook in which I had written a question per page and an attempt at an answer. There must have been 100 or so questions in there to review and 'revise'.

Her initial response, as I handed over the book so that she could quiz me, was 'What the f**k is that?' 'My revision book, my questions and answers,' I said. She replied with an eye roll and a 'Wow'.

She then showed me a better way.

It is impossible to know what questions you might get asked and to try to prepare for every eventuality is exhausting and probably worthless.

The approach she showed me, which I now use with all my coaching clients, is about creating a set of case studies for yourself which cover a variety of angles and which you can immediately refer to when asked a question.

Let me explain. When looking at a job description and getting ready for an interview you will likely see the type of person they are looking for and can assume a certain level of questioning on some subjects.

For example:

An HR director role

People management
Organisational skills
Project management
Cost saving / Restructuring / Org redesign

Instead of thinking of ALL the questions around those subjects, think of 4–6 case studies which illustrate the points.

- An example where you managed a large team, dealt with difficulty, did a restructure
- An example of a successful project where you saved money, implemented a new IT system, dealt with difficult stakeholders
- An example of a challenging project which shows org redesign, people management, delays and overspend

 **Exercise**

Case Study Planning

To make it easier you can use a grid or a table:

Case Study Planner

Operational leadership Day-to-Day KPIs Performance Management	Project where I restructured department Vision Strategy Selling it	Issue with PMs Had to fire someone Fill gaps and get new resources
500k budget Did business case Senior leaders and buy-in Managed stakeholders Sold benefits	**Key skills needed** Project management People leadership Budget Difficult decisions?	Decision on redundancy Decision to stop one stream of project Streamlining management team
People Future talent Recruitment / Retention involvement	Managed 100 people Coaching - set up new programme Difficult messages Selling change	Setting up structures Budget reporting Escalations process Complaints

Case Study Planner

Stories

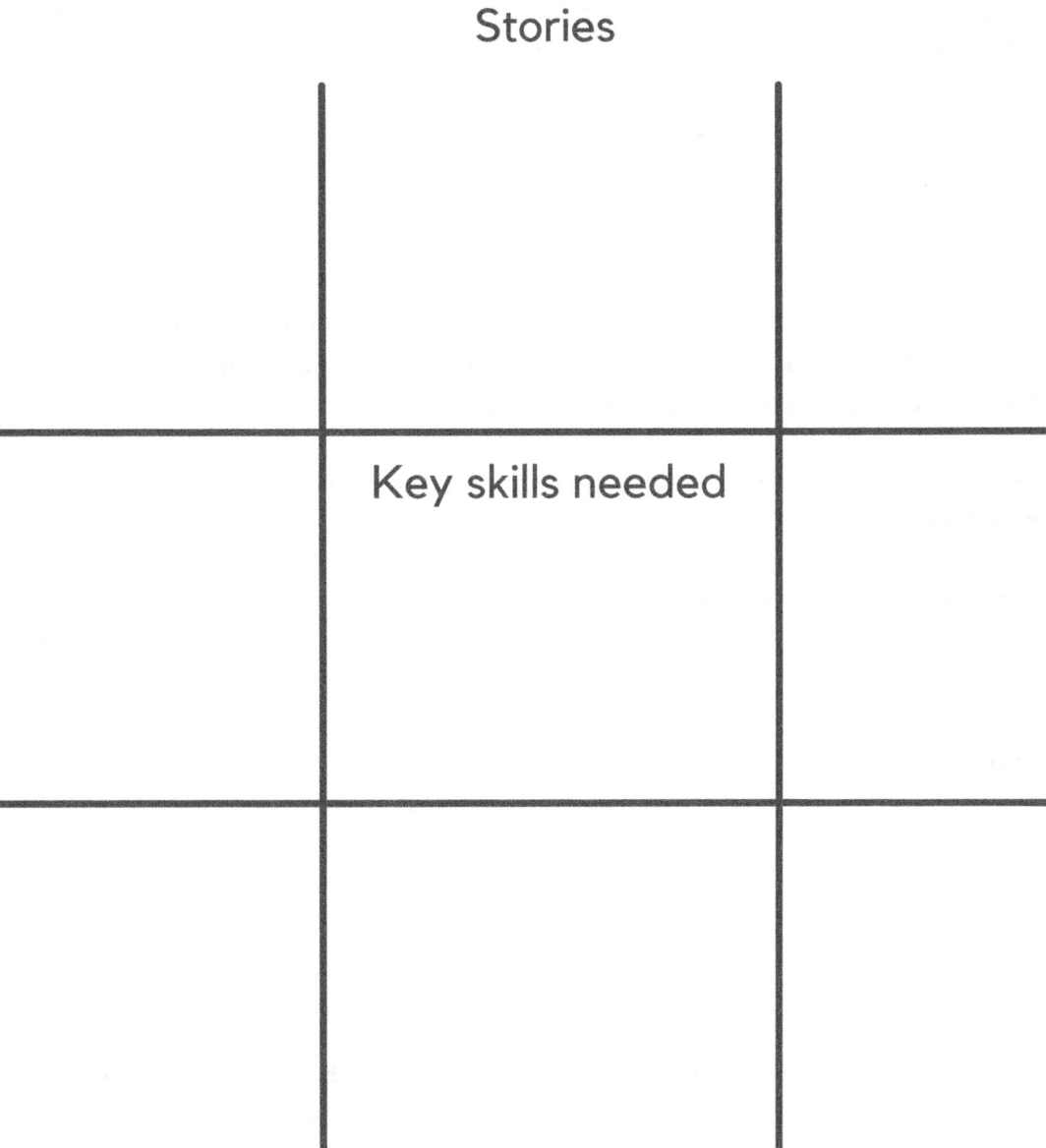

Key skills needed

Once you have worked out the job requirements, and the skills required, you can start to think of your examples. These might have already been listed in your CV but when you think a little deeper there might be some other more illustrative examples or stories which show how you overcame a challenge, or motivated a team, or negotiated with senior stakeholders.

So, you can write those down and see which boxes they tick. What requirements is that example illustrating? At this stage, list ALL the good examples you have.

It's also a good time to think about any negatives that might come up if pressed. And you might decide to cull that example.

For example:

If you did implement a large project which shows some of the skills, but it overran and went over budget, you might want to choose another example which shows your skills in a better light. The follow-up question might make that example inappropriate.

Once you have a list you can then start to review and hone the top 4–6 items. What you are looking for here is the strongest examples that can cover multiple angles.

For example: Organising a restructure

Headlines:

Large restructure of multiple departments
Off shored various teams
Redundancy programme

Internal organisation redesign
Stakeholder buy-in
Budget management

Not only does it show that you managed the restructure itself well, but it can also be used in response to a question about people leadership and senior stakeholder management. Potentially it can also be the example you turn to about budget management, problems uncovered and challenges faced.

Explore all the angles.

Then in the interview when asked:

'Can you give me an example where you have had to manage challenging stakeholders?' or
'Can you give me some details on a successful restructure that you carried out, and what were the pitfalls?' you can call upon the same example but from a different angle.

It is important to have several really good examples showing a variety of skills because if you always use the same case study, you'll look like a one-trick pony! Have several that you know really, really well and then you can dip in and out.

In the case of another question:

'Can you give me an example where you had to manage a tight budget and tight deadlines?' you'll need to think. Yes, the restructure example could be used but you don't want to overuse it.

You can always say: *'Obviously the big restructure was a good example of that, but I also did it in my other role at xxx Ltd and there I had a smaller budget and the requirement was to...'*

You are showing there that you have multiple examples but you're going to pick another one to demonstrate for them.

In your case studies, list what they were, what the facts and figures were, but don't forget why you were the one to get those results. What you did to manage the project, what skills you want to highlight.

It was your great negotiation skills that got the organisation out of a hole.
It was your personal touch and empathy that meant that a tribunal was avoided.
It was your strategic vision that saw a new way and saved large sums of money.
It was your presentation skills that got it over the line at a board meeting.

Go back to the Natural Talents Exercise; what key skills do you want to demonstrate? Are they featured in all your case studies? If not, add them. Add the depth and the flavour of you to the case studies.

Once you have written them all down and picked your best 4–6 stories (plus any specific examples), start by saying them out loud. Tell that story to someone else or if that feels too weird, just talk it out to an empty room or into your phone. You'll be amazed at what else you remember by doing this.

Bring the story to life. Focus on what YOU did, what YOU achieved and what the RESULTS were for the organisation.

Avoid

Any politics
The history lesson — no-one needs the back story or the whys and wherefores
Any bad blood
Any dissing of the previous organisation or their management — you want to show professionalism
Too much detail
Anything that would breach confidentiality clauses

So now you should have 4–6 strong detailed case studies which highlight your skills and the requirements of the role in a number of ways.

Specific interview questions

For some roles there will always be the specific questions that require a specific answer, and some preparation will be required for those.

Have you ever had to manage someone through a disciplinary?

Either you have or you haven't, or you may have done a hundred. Either way, if it is a key part of the role then you should prepare for the response, especially if you have no experience. You might only have one case study you can draw on for that, but it is worth preparing.

'Why are you leaving your current place of work?'

It might be that you dislike your manager. But now is NOT the time to say that.

Think around the issues and look at the positives of why you want to move to this organisation.

PUSH factors – the reasons why you want to leave

- Look at the Dream Job Mind Map Exercise — there are reasons here that are personal to you
- Maybe you wanted a shorter commute, and this role is closer

- Maybe you wanted less politics — this can be framed as going to a place where you will be more empowered
- Culture change
- Hours
- Locations
- Explore those reasons and find the most compelling one where you can speak honestly, openly and without blame

PULL factors — the reasons why you want to join them

- Look at why you applied
- What was it about them specifically that you loved?
- What sparked an interest?
- What positives can you refer to about their brand that appealed?

You can then start to piece together your own particular response.

For example:

'I have been looking for a new opportunity where I have more responsibility for a while, and when this role came up, I could see that this organisation's culture was a great match.'

Or

'During lockdown I have really enjoyed working from home with no commute and so this role with its more flexible approach was really appealing.'

Be prepared for the questions about gaps, inexperience, and lack of skills.

What if you have gaps in your CV where you were not working? Ideally you will have explained the gaps and what you did during any period where you were not employed. Employers may still like to drill into those areas.

Acknowledge that you have the gap in employment. You are not trying to blag it. Outline what you did and the skills you learnt during that period that are relevant (if appropriate).

If you have skills gaps you may also be asked questions. If you are new to management or budgets, for example, you might need to acknowledge that you have limited (or no) experience but are doing x, y and z to get up to speed or will be keen to learn. You might say that you are a quick learner and use an example where you had to take on additional responsibility at short notice and how you went about learning. Think about where you might have done any networking, shadowing others, reading books, going on courses, having a mentor that can support this.

It can also lead you to ask them some questions:

'As I am new to this area what support would I get to help bring me up to speed?'

'Are there any mentor programmes that I could use to help me get the skills more quickly?'

Specific Interview Questions

What interview questions do you know will come up for you?

Consider the following topic areas:

- Experience
- Reason for leaving
- Gaps in CV
- Specific industry requirements
- Qualifications / Training

Make a note of any questions that come up.

_____

_____

_____

_____

Take time to prepare your response using the examples.

Make any notes of ideas for your responses below:

_____
_____
_____
_____

Exercise

Key Date Planner

What dates are relevant to your search now?

_____
_____
_____
_____
_____
_____

Things to consider:

- What is your ideal new start date?
- What is your notice period (if any)?
- When is your first available start date (it's good to have this in your mind before you start the interview process)?
- When will you do your interview preparation work?
- What gap do you want between roles? (if relevant)

 **Summary**

Presenting your best self at interview means being prepared, being confident and being organised, ready to share your most interesting and relevant stories.

Make sure you have:

1. Reviewed the top tips
2. Planned ahead for your interview — whether face to face or online
3. Reviewed your best stories and case studies that can answer multiple questions
4. Prepared for the standard questions
5. Prepared for the specific questions
6. Prepared your own questions for the interviewer

Chapter 15

Accepting the offers (or not)

BY NOW YOU'LL be in the swing of assessing your applications, researching your target companies, going confidently for interviews. Now — what to do when you get those offers?

Should I stay or should I go?

At this stage it is all about weighing up the positives versus the negatives. It's highly unlikely that 100% of your **ideal job checklist** is going to be met. However, you will have put in the range of what you will and won't accept against the various categories you want to weigh up. Time to get the list out and review!

Saying 'no' with confidence

It's important that even at this stage you remember that you can still walk away. But that can feel daunting.

How do you feel saying 'no' to someone? Do you feel confident in asking for what you want?

If you're OK with both these statements, feel free to skip on.

But for many of us the idea of saying 'no' might fill us with dread. Turning down a job can be just as daunting as applying for one. And going back and asking for a better package can also make us feel awful.

Having your **ideal job checklist** is a major plus here.

You won't need to think of excuses; you can simply say something like:
'Since doing more research / having the interview I can see that this role is not a good match for what I am looking for.'

If asked you can elaborate with more detail:
'It was advertised as flexible but in reality, the manager wanted more hours.'
'I want to be local, however there is a lot more travel than I can commit to.'
'I found that the culture of the organisation wasn't a good match for me; I am looking for x and y.'

Saying no to interviews

When you applied for the job, you thought it was a great match, but since you sent in your application there is something that is not feeling right. Perhaps it is the process they are asking you to follow which is indicative of a culture you're not keen on. Maybe you've spoken to some friends who have filled you in on the real story. You may simply have already found your dream job. You'll need to make a call to explain why you are no longer applying.

Before the call:

- Stick to the facts each time — you don't need to lie or make the recruiter feel good.
- Make a note of the key points beforehand and have them with you when you call.
- Do the power pose exercise so that you are physically feeling better.
- Be polite — you might need them next time.
- If asked, feel free to give them feedback — you could help the next person who is applying there. For example:
    - *'The role was advertised saying "flexible working considered" but what I wanted wasn't considered.'*
- If this one of the reasons you applied but in reality, when interviewed you found that the flexibility on offer was limited or lacking, then giving this feedback to the recruiter or agency could be helpful.

Saying no to offers

You went to the interview and now you have an offer to consider. After you've reviewed it with your **ideal job checklist** you've decided that this role is one to decline. Ask yourself, are you saying an 'absolute no' or are you wanting more from the offer?

Absolute no

- Using your **ideal job checklist**, work out what reason you are specifically declining for if you can.
- Stick to the facts each time — you don't need to lie or make the recruiter feel good.
- Make a note of the key points beforehand and have them with you when you call.
- Do the power pose exercise so that you are physically feeling better.
- Be polite — you might need them next time.
- Thank them for the offer.
- If you have chosen an alternative offer, they might ask what that offer was, and what it was about it that made you say yes. Consider whether you would like to share — you don't have to but it might help them to improve for the next person.

A 'no for now'

If you are wanting to say 'no' to negotiate, consider the risk of doing this. By saying 'no', you may risk them accepting that and moving on to the next person.

A different way might be to say, *'I'd love to have said yes, but there is something I can't accept about the offer'*, and then go on to explain the sticking point. That way they know you are keen, and they are also very clear on what you want.

By using your **ideal job checklist**, you'll know what you will and won't accept.

Saying YES

For some saying yes will be a nerve-racking experience. This might be a very big move. This is your dream job after all!

Remember to go back to your **ideal job checklist** and make sure that you are getting what you want and that you are happy with any compromises. Don't just feel like you have to accept the first thing that comes along, or the first offer.

Tune in: How does the offer make you feel?

Does it offer all the things you want?

Is there anything at all you are unsure of?

Are you happy to accept the compromises (if any)?

_____

_____

_____

How happy will you be if you take this offer?

_____

_____

_____

_____

On a scale of 1 to 10, score how you feel right now about the job offer you have.

1	2	3	4	5	6	7	8	9	10
It feels off				OK					It can't be better

Take a moment to recognise what it is about your own talents and skills that has got you the role.

When saying yes:

- Take time to check all the points in the contract and offer
- Make sure you have covered all areas of your package that you want
- Don't be blinded by excitement
- Ask any culture related questions that you want reassurance about – such as flexible working practices in reality
- Write down any questions in advance and make sure you tick them off
- Show how keen you are
- Say thanks to the recruiter

The offer is only the first step; be sure to follow up with all of the various bits of paperwork that follow. This is the dream job. You don't want to have your offer withdrawn because you didn't get the contract back in time (I have seen this happen).

 # Case Study

Josie

Josie recently got her dream job and was excited to tell me how she had negotiated her salary.

She was pleased because she had felt that she had done so badly at previous attempts at negotiating that she really wanted to do it well this time.

Using the ideal job checklist helped because it meant that she already had the list of what she wanted and what her package requirements were, which meant that she was forearmed before she took the call.

'I really decided to back myself,' she said. 'I had done my research and I knew what I was worth. It wasn't just about the money... the culture and their approach to flexibility was really important. So, at each stage of the process, whether it was the interview or the follow-up calls, making the offer or negotiating the details, I made sure I kept talking about those key elements. I knew that I would walk away if it didn't sound right and that gave me power.'

'Knowing my current package in detail was really useful. In my old role I was entitled to a guaranteed bonus; I made sure I mentioned that I would be losing out on that in the negotiations and ended up getting a two-year sign-on bonus to compensate for the bonus I'd have missed out on.'

Knowing exactly what your package is worth in the future can be really useful; it's not just about the value today.

'If I had my time again, I think I would have done even more preparation,' Josie continued. 'It really is the key. I forgot to ask about a training programme that I really wanted, and I know will be valuable in the role. I will ask once I am in, but I would have been better off asking before I signed. I also didn't think to find out about whether you could buy holiday — with young children that would have been a good thing but in the end the process happened really quickly. I'd encourage people to ask for a bit of breathing space, just so you don't forget something crucial.'

Leaving well

Whatever the reason for leaving, make sure you leave your organisation well.

It's a small world out there and you never know who you might meet in the future.

You can resign well and do a good handover and leave without bitterness and resentment. In my experience those negative emotions only stick with us anyway!

The more senior you are, the more likely this will require some good planning and organisation. You may well find that you are involved in hiring your own replacement if time and politics allows.

Planning your exit

- Make sure you have resigned via the correct channels
- Have a clear understanding of your leave date — including whether you can take holiday or will have it paid
- Meet with your manager and discuss what needs to be done before you leave or what they would like you to hand over by when and to whom. Ask about when and how your team (if you have one) should be briefed
- Agree up front what you will and won't get involved in, which meetings you should continue attending and which you no longer need to go to

Taking action

- Be sure to do what you've said you will
- Flag up anything that cannot be done or any blockers that get in the way of you delivering
- Tidy up your own task lists and finish things off well
- Find people to hand over tasks and work to
- Teach people what you know

If you know that you did your best when leaving then that is all you can do. If others are not interested in taking things from you, or don't hear what you are saying, then that is on them. You will have done what you could to ensure a controlled and planned exit. You can only control what you can control.

Be gracious when you are asked not to attend certain meetings; you are now someone who is leaving and are not part of the future. Time to take a step back and tidy up whatever else remains before you leave.

Reflect on the good connections you have made, and make sure you take details so you can keep in touch and then start to focus on your new future.

Exercise

Key Date Planner

You are now getting ready to accept a role and start your new one.

Make a note of anything to do right now:

_____

_____

_____

_____

Things to consider:

- What do you need to do before you leave?
- What do you need to do before you start?
- What dates are you now working to?

New start date: _____

Remaining notice period (if any): _____

Holiday to be taken / Gap between roles: _____

_____

 **Summary**

You've come so far, now you only want to accept the right roles for you.

Make sure you:

1. Consider how the new role and offers feel — do they feel right?

2. Use your **ideal job checklist** to tick off whether each role is a good fit.

3. Get confident saying yes and no.

4. Leave positively.

Chapter 16

Congratulations

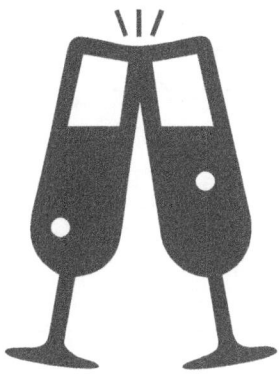

WELL DONE!!!!

You now have your dream job!!

Take a moment to reflect! Take some time to congratulate yourself!

 **Exercise**

Reflection

Look back at all of the exercises you have done during this process.

What have you learnt about yourself?

_____

_____

_____

_____

_____

_____

What have you learnt about how work fits into your life right now?

_____

_____

_____

_____

_____

_____

What do you want to take forward from this process into your life when the job starts?

___

Boundaries – new for your new role and new life

It's a great achievement, getting a new role that is a better fit for the life you want right now.

Before you start the job, it can be really helpful to set out any boundaries or 'rules' that you want to embed and adopt so that you maintain the way of working you want from the start.

Consider what it was about the old job and your old way of working that you wanted to change.

How will you make sure that you don't slip into any old habits in the new role?

How will you notice if things don't feel aligned for you in the future?

What indicators might you set for yourself so you can monitor whether the job remains a good fit?

Make any notes here to remind yourself.

_____

_____

_____

_____

_____

A coaching client of mine does a weekly review against the checklist items that were important to them. Long hours and health issues were a concern, so they set out their own boundaries around end-of-day times and putting in time to exercise. Each week they plan ahead to ensure that they have exercise scheduled in and also have clear 'stop' times each day. Then on a Friday they review how successful they have been at achieving this. They can start to see any 'creep' very quickly and make adjustments.

Another coaching client wanting a more flexible solution made sure that at the very start of their employment they spoke to their team about the hours they were contracted to do, so there was full transparency. They highlighted what to do in an emergency and what constituted an emergency in the first place! They decided to put a footer on their emails so it was clear to everyone. When asked to attend an all-day meeting on their non-working day, they were able to remind the person that they didn't work that day, because it was all out in the open.

What would your ideal week or month look like?

Use the time planner to start to shape your new week in your new role.

 # Exercise

Time Planner

Use this planner to think about your ideal week. When do you want to start and end your work day, and what other elements require planning in?

Things to consider

Exercise, sleep, food, family time, commuting, school runs, dog walks, blocks of work time, regular meetings, travel, hobbies, social, thinking time.

Weekly	Mon	Tues	Weds	Thurs	Fri	Sat	Sun
4am							
5am							
6am							
7am							
8am							
9am							
10am							
11am							
12 noon							
1pm							
2pm							
3pm							
4pm							
5pm							
6pm							
7pm							
8pm							
9pm							
10pm							
11pm							
12 midnight							

You can also look at your work schedule a month ahead — this can be especially useful for regular monthly meeting planning such as finance reports, customer deadlines and other regular items. It can be helpful for delegating tasks. If you know the monthly finance meeting is on the third Thursday of the month, then asking your direct reports for the data you need by the third Monday can give you the time you need to prepare your information.

Things to consider

Leadership meetings, team meetings, budget meetings and deadlines, board meetings and paper deadlines, 121s, WFH days, holidays, bank holidays, expenses and other regular paperwork, strategic thinking, away days.

Monthly		Mon	Tues	Weds	Thurs	Fri
Week 1	Morning					
	Afternoon					
Week 2	Morning					
	Afternoon					
Week 3	Morning					
	Afternoon					
Week 4	Morning					
	Afternoon					
Week 5	Morning					
	Afternoon					

Case Study

Helen

'A key element for me getting a new role in a new area after having my baby was the fact that I could look for something and somewhere completely different. I saw people returning to work in my old company and there was no change in the expectations that people had of you. If you used to work long hours, then they'd expect the same even though you now had to leave to get to nursery. I saw people really struggling so when I was working on my ideal job checklist I knew that the family-friendly policies and culture would be higher up the list.

'When I went for an interview with the organisation I am with now, the two women who interviewed me actually said "You've had a baby; things will be different now and that is OK". They knew that the baby could be ill or there could be issues and they said that they expected that; they'd been there themselves and they gave me permission to have as much flexibility as I needed.

'I found a new start was just what I needed personally. I could wipe the slate clean and develop my own new timetable and routine and set my new boundaries for this stage of my life.'

 **Exercise**

Post Job Review

You've got the job and you've been in the role for a couple of months. It can be helpful to review how you feel now. For some contracts when your probation period concludes it can lead to longer notice periods. So, if you are not happy then review and react now before you are tied into a longer notice period.

Even though you did all of the prep work and made a really informed choice about the organisation, the role, what it was going to offer you, sometimes the job is not what was advertised.

We can still arrive at a place, and it simply is not what was sold to us, or not as it seemed at interview. If you can review and take action or speak up now, then things might be able to be changed. Or if it can't be changed then you have a very solid reason to say no when the probation review is up.

Now is the time to sit and think about the role.

On a scale of 1 to 10, score how you feel right now about the job.

1	2	3	4	5	6	7	8	9	10
It's as bad as it can be				OK					Can't be better

Make a note along the line.

Go back to your **ideal job checklist** — is everything being met as expected?

If the score is high, the **ideal job checklist** is being met and you feel great, then this is excellent. Acknowledge that feeling and recognise that this is an excellent job, in a great place, and you feel good about it right now.

What is going well?

_____
_____
_____
_____
_____

What do you love?

_____
_____
_____
_____
_____

What is your body telling you?

_____
_____
_____
_____
_____

If the scores are a little lower than you hoped for, the **ideal job checklist** has some missing elements, or you are not feeling as good about it, then it is time to reflect. Take a few minutes with no distractions to think about what is going on.

What specifically is missing / wrong?

_____

_____

_____

What are the missing elements of the **ideal job checklist**?

_____

_____

_____

What is not as good as was promised?

_____

_____

_____

What is your body telling you?

_____

_____

_____

What is different to what you were expecting?

_____

_____

_____

Now you have some ideas about what it might be:

Is there something you can do about it?

As we've discovered it can take a long time to search for and find a job. Is there something that you can discuss now to get resolved?

Who can you talk to?

_____

_____

_____

Is the issue work related or more related to home or the family set-up?

_____

_____

_____

What might you be able to change yourself?

_____

_____

_____

Are there changes you can make to boundaries / how you have set up your day?

What would you say to your manager if you were asked?

What would you need help with?

What do you conclude from this process?

Is this job 'good enough' to keep and try to adjust to? Or is it one to walk away from? You always have a choice.

_____

_____

_____

_____

Re-use and re-use again

The beauty of this process is that you can use it again and again.

Our lives and circumstances change all the time. The choices I made for my career when my children were tiny are different to the choices I make now when they are a lot older. The choices I needed to make when my health was poor were at a certain point in time. Then my health improved and I could do different activities and I had more energy for my career. Life is in constant flux, and the choices you might make now for your current life circumstances might change in six months or three years' time. Come back to this book when you need to. It might be:

- To review this job in three months or one year's time
- To review an internal promotion or job changes
- To review how you feel about your life
- To review where your slice of life is right now
- To restart the process after a life change

 **Summary**

You've got the role; it's time to celebrate!

Make sure you:

1. Celebrate and reflect on your achievements

2. Think about what you have learnt

3. Consider any new boundaries for the new role

4. Review the new role in a few weeks' time to check in with how it feels

Chapter 17

More case studies

HERE ARE A few more case studies that you might find useful. You can also find other more recent case studies on my website www.dellajudd.co.uk/bookresources.

Leia

Leia was a student who was looking for her first proper job after finishing her A levels. She was lacking in confidence and thought she had no experience and no stories to tell. After a conversation she realised that she had a lot to talk about — she just hadn't thought of things that way.

I asked her:

What sort of projects did you do at school?

How did they go?

Who did you work with?

Was there anyone difficult that you had to deal with? How did you manage working with that person?

Did you have to work as a team on that project? How did you organise yourself?

What worked? What didn't work?

How well did she manage her time and planning for exams? She was very good at this and in fact had helped a friend to organise themselves.

I asked, on what other areas did your friends come to you for help? How did you help them? Why do you think they asked you?

What do you do to help you concentrate? How would that help you in a workplace?

What subjects did she study? What did she think might be relevant about those subjects in the role that she went for? This could be statistics, analysis, writing reports, attention to detail, being creative, designing new ideas, thinking about the wider world, thinking about other people.

What did she do for fun outside of school? What hobbies did she have?
Was she a member of any clubs?
Did she play music or take part in any sports?

What could she learn about the discipline of those that could help her? How did she manage her time with a busy schedule?

Was she part of any committees?

Was she a prefect? Did she have any responsibility, such as a librarian or reading to juniors?

Was there any time when things had gone wrong for her? Had a project gone wrong, had she missed a deadline? How did she feel when overcoming those challenges?

What did she do about that situation? How did she escalate it when it went wrong?

I asked her why she had applied for the job and what it was that was of interest. She spoke passionately without rehearsing. This was her true honest answer. I told her that she should speak exactly like that at interview. Speak from the heart.

I asked her, of the skills and attributes that we had discovered by asking the questions above, what was it that she now thought she would bring to the role? She realised that she had lots of skills in areas such as organisation, proactiveness, taking responsibility and being creative that would be useful.

By the end of the session, she was realising that by digging a little deeper into what she had done and how she had managed things, she had a lot more to say than she thought. She felt more confident armed with those answers and that information.

Mason

Mason approached me after recent organisational changes left him feeling vulnerable. Whilst he was a senior decision maker, it was clear to him that wholesale changes were happening, and he wasn't sure that he would be safe. He was a new dad and was looking for more security as well as continuing a strong career progression.

Mason realised the culture of his current organisation was a far cry from the organisation he had previously been in. Both had their challenges. He didn't want to make a mistake and didn't want to move somewhere radical just to jump away from the current situation.

We explored what it was he liked about both roles. And we also spent a lot of time exploring what he did not like. We then looked at the culture.

What was it about the set-up of each organisation that was beneficial and then conversely what was a challenge?

Mason identified that the two organisations were wildly different. One was a partnership set-up, with multiple owners and therefore multiple directions. It was well respected which he liked but the politics were high. The second organisation was a global corporate with multiple structures. Decision making was clearer, but also run from a global perspective. Those decisions were made at a global level, so sometimes local nuance was being missed. Financially it was run extremely tightly and there was little room for investment in areas such as culture, wellbeing, and development.

Once we had established what was going on, Mason could create his own checklist which included stability, more local decision making and influence, investment and interest in culture, wellbeing and development.

Felicia

Felicia came to me when she had been singled out with a NDA and a 'tap on the shoulder' that her role was no longer viable.

She was devastated. Initially her focus was on getting a new job, but it became clear that to move on she needed first to deal with the emotions that she was feeling as a result of being let down by her organisation.

She was finding it difficult to focus, to work out what she wanted. Her confidence was at an all-time low. She was doubting herself and wondering 'Is it me?' She had difficulty in articulating what she was good at because the previous experience had sapped her of her energy.

Slowly but surely, we progressed through the exercises, looking at what positives she could take from the past experiences. What had gone well? What could she retell about her story that didn't start with negativity, anger, and upset?

She wanted to completely change tack, drop down a level or two and restart doing something different. She was worried about what other people would say, so we worked on the new 'story' she would tell her friends and family that she could feel comfortable with.

We did the Dream Job Mind Map Exercise; we did a CV review to focus it on the new role she wanted rather than the old role she had. Slowly I saw her confidence start to increase, and she started to apply for roles which were a good cultural fit. It took some time, because her nerves were still there, but by applying for roles she knew were a good fit it started to rebuild her self-esteem.

About the author

DELLA IS AN inspirational leader who has coached and mentored hundreds of people in the last 25 years in her senior roles at Deloitte, KPMG, Invensys, Elsevier and British Gas. Her personal experiences with burnout, redundancy, childcare, mental health and stress have made her the coach she is today. She has seen first-hand the importance of valuing mental health, flexible working, and parenthood in the workplace.

Della is passionate about helping people to discover what they truly desire from a job, and to help them to achieve just that, getting the job and the balance that is right for them right now.

Della has inspired many people to realise how much they are capable of, how to be confident and to keep pushing to get the life of their dreams. Her inspirational, encouraging, and positive voice shines through as your helpful guide to making sure you *Get the Job You Really Want.*

As a career coach she uses her unique approach to help people to get to the heart of what they really want in life, to help them with their own personal job search.

How she can help you:

- Helping people get the job they really want — career coaching with a difference
- Supporting people with burnout — helping them to return to work
- Helping leavers to leave well — bespoke outplacement for senior redundancies/retirements
- Coaching maternity returners to navigate their way back to work successfully

Get in touch

www.dellajudd.co.uk

www.dellajudd.co.uk/bookresources

Della Judd | LinkedIn

https://www.linkedin.com/in/della-judd-50256942/

Via email: admin@DellaJudd.co.uk

Bonus chapters and free stuff!

You can access additional material, more case studies and view free webinars via my website:

www.dellajudd.co.uk/bookresources

www.ingramcontent.com/pod-product-compliance
Lightning Source LLC
Chambersburg PA
CBHW080345300426
44110CB00019B/2508